A.V. Dice

A Leap in the Dark

A.V. Dicey

A Leap in the Dark

1st Edition | ISBN: 978-3-75230-876-1

Place of Publication: Frankfurt am Main, Germany

Year of Publication: 2020

Outlook Verlag GmbH, Germany.

Reproduction of the original.

A Leap in the Dark

By A.V. Dicey

Introduction

Irish Unionists have pressed for a republication of *A Leap in the Dark*. They hold that it will be of some service in their resistance to the Coalition of Home Rulers, Socialists, and Separatists formed to force upon the people of England and of Scotland a virtual dissolution of the Union between Great Britain and Ireland. It would in any case have been a pleasure to afford aid, however small, to the Irish Unionists, whether Protestants or Catholics, engaged in the defence at once of their own birthright and of the political unity of the United Kingdom. Yet for a moment I doubted whether the republication of a forgotten criticism of a forgotten Bill would be of essential service to my friends. On reflection, however, I have come to see that, though the Unionists of Ireland probably overrate the practical value of my book, yet their hope of its serving the cause whereof they are the most valiant defenders is based on sound reasons.

A Leap in the Dark is a stringent criticism of the Home Rule Bill, 1893.[1] But the book has little to do with the details and intricacies of that Bill. *A Leap in the Dark* was published before the Home Rule Bill of 1893 had reached the House of Lords, or had assumed that final form, which made patent to the vast majority of British electors that a measure which purported to give a limited amount of independence to Ireland, in reality threatened England with political ruin. My criticism is therefore in truth an attack upon the fundamental principles of Home Rule, as advocated by Gladstone and his followers eighteen years ago. These principles, moreover, have never been repudiated by the Home Rulers of to-day. Some members of the present Cabinet, notably the Prime Minister and Lord Morley, were the apologists of the Bill of 1893. In that year *A Leap in the Dark, or Our New Constitution*, was, I venture to say, accepted by leading Unionists, such as Lord Salisbury, the Duke of Devonshire, Mr. Balfour, Mr. Chamberlain, Sir Henry James (now Lord James of Hereford), as, in the main, an adequate representation of the objections which, in the judgment of such men and thousands of Unionists, were fatal to the acceptance of any scheme whatever of Home Rule for Ireland. The battle over Home Rule lasting, as it did for years, and ending with the complete victory of the Unionists, has been forgotten by or has never become known to the mass of the present electors. It is well that they should be reminded of the solid grounds for the rejection by the Lords of the Home Rule Bill of 1893. It is well that they should be reminded that this rejection was in 1895 ratified by the approval of the electorate of the United Kingdom *A Leap in the Dark* will assuredly remind my readers that in 1893 the hereditary House of Lords, and not the newly elected House of Commons, truly represented the will of the nation. This is a fact never to be forgotten. It is of special import at the present moment. Another equally undoubted fact deserves attention. Home Rulers themselves despair of carrying a Home Rule Bill until they shall have turned the Parliament Bill into the Parliament Act, 1911, and my readers ought never to forget that the passing of the Parliament Bill into law destroys, and is meant to destroy, every security against the passing of any Home Rule Bill whatever which the present majority of the House of Commons choose to support. This gives an ominous significance to the obstinate refusal of the Government to alter or amend any of the material enactments contained in this ill-starred measure. *A Leap in the Dark*, combined with a knowledge of the Parliament Bill and the legislative dictatorship with which it invests the existing Coalition, suggests at least four conclusions which must at all costs be forced at this moment upon the attention of the nation. They may be thus summed up:

First.—If the Parliament Bill passes into law the existing majority of the House of Commons will be able to force, and will assuredly in fact force, through Parliament any Home Rule Bill whatever (even were it the Home Rule Bill of 1893), which meets with the approval of Mr. Redmond, and obtains the acquiescence of the rest of the Coalition.

The Coalition need not fear any veto of the House of Lords. There will be no necessity for an appeal to the electors, or in other words to the nation. The truth of this statement is indisputable. The legal right of the majority of the House of Commons to pass any bill whatever into law, even though the House of Lords refuse its assent, is absolutely secured by the very terms of the Parliament Bill. That the leaders of the Coalition, such as Mr. Asquith, the Chancellor of the Exchequer, and Mr. John Redmond, will press their legal right to its extreme limits is proved to any man who knows how to read the teaching of history, by the experience of 1893. Mr. Gladstone used every power he possessed, and used it unscrupulously, to drive a Home Rule Bill through the House of Commons. He was a man trained in the historical traditions of Parliament. He assuredly did not relish the use of the closure and the guillotine. He was supported in the Commons by a very narrow majority, never I think exceeding forty-eight, and often falling below that number. The power of the party system, or as Americans say, the "Machine," was admittedly much less in 1893 than it has become in 1911. Yet Mr. Gladstone used such power as he possessed to the utmost. He hurried through the House of Commons a Bill which had not in fact received the assent of the nation. He made the freest use of every device for curtailing freedom of debate. A large and most important portion of the Home Rule Bill was not discussed at all in the Commons. And this Bill contained provisions, not appearing in its original form, for the retention of eighty Irish members at Westminster with full

3

authority to take part in every kind of legislation which might be laid before Parliament; though Mr. Gladstone himself held the fairness to England of this provision dubious[2] and Mr. (now Lord) Morley had in 1886 demonstrated by reasoning which to my mind is absolutely conclusive that under a system of Home Rule the presence of Irish representatives in the Imperial Parliament at Westminster would work fatal injury to Ireland and gross injustice to England.[3] Can any man able to draw from political precedents their true meaning believe that Mr. Asquith, and the allies who are his masters, will be more scrupulous in forcing the next Home Rule Bill through the House of Lords than was Mr. Gladstone in forcing the Home Rule Bill of 1893 through the House of Commons? Mr. Asquith is supported by a large though incongruous majority. His almost avowed aim in pushing the Parliament Bill, unchanged and unchangeable, through the Houses of Parliament is to force the Home Rule Bill on the people of Great Britain against their will. Hesitation to make use of this dictatorial authority, should he ever obtain it, will to himself mean political ruin; to his English supporters it will seem political pusillanimity; by his Irish confederates it will be denounced as breach of faith and treachery. As certainly as night follows day the passing of the Parliament Act will be succeeded by the attempted passing of a Home Rule Act.

Secondly.—Mr. Redmond and the Home Rulers, or Separatists, of whom he is the leader, will exact under any Home Rule Bill of say 1912 or 1913, at lowest, every advantage which was demanded by Irish Nationalists in 1893.

Why, in the name of common sense, when Irish Nationalists are absolute masters of the situation, should they demand lower payment for their support than was offered to them twenty years ago when the Home Rule majority was every day losing strength, when every one knew that nothing but the show of moderation gave the slightest chance of a Home Rule Bill escaping the veto of the House of Lords, when every one, except perhaps Mr. Gladstone, foresaw that the next General Election would give to Unionists a crushing majority? Every advantage conceded in 1893 to Irish Separatists at the expense of England will assuredly reappear in one form or another in the next Home Rule Bill. Thus Ireland will, we may anticipate, under the next Home Rule Bill send to the Parliament at Westminster at least eighty members armed with the fullest legislative authority, so that, to revive the language current eighteen years ago, Ireland will govern and tax England whilst England will retain no right either to govern or to tax Ireland.

Thirdly.—Every question to which in 1893 Gladstonians could discover no answer satisfactory to Unionists or to the electorate of Great Britain requires an answer in 1911 as much as in 1893. The answer favourable to Home Rule

4

has not as yet been discovered.

Is it possible to combine the effective supremacy of the Imperial Parliament with Home Rule or the substantial legislative independence of Ireland? Can Ireland, close to the shore of Great Britain, occupy the position of a self-governing colony, such as New Zealand, divided from Great Britain by thousands of miles of sea? Is it possible to create, or even to imagine, a Court which shall decide whether a law passed by the Irish Parliament violates the provisions of the proposed Home Rule Act? Above all, can the wit of man devise any scheme of constitution which shall at once satisfy the aspirations of Irish Nationalism and the patently just demand of Ulster that Protestants shall retain the freedom and the rights secured to them as citizens of the United Kingdom? Is there any form of Home Rule which will satisfy the desire of Irish Nationalists for something approaching national independence without the urgent peril of rousing civil war between Ulster and the Parliament at Dublin? All these inquiries, and others like them, harassed the Parliament of 1893; they were all answered by Unionists, that is by the majority of the British electors, with a decided negative; they will all be raised and will all need an answer when the leaders of the Coalition condescend to produce their next Home Rule Bill or even to reveal its fundamental principles.

Fourthly.—England in the circumstances of to-day is threatened with two perils which did not exist in 1893, and yet are of stupendous gravity.

The first is, that in the case of a measure of Home Rule the opportunities for discussing its provisions which are contained in the Parliament Bill may turn out nominal rather than real. It is not at all certain that for such a Bill, even though it be abhorred by the electorate of the United Kingdom, the House of Lords will be practically able to secure the delay and elaborate discussion to which Mr. Asquith professedly attaches immense importance. Unionists will believe that the measure passed by a large majority of the House of Commons is detested by the majority of the British electors. But how will it be possible to carry on the government of Ireland, to maintain order, or to save a loyal minority from gross oppression after a Home Rule Bill applauded by Separatists has been passed through the House of Commons, and for the first time has been rejected by the House of Lords? Every official in Ireland, down from the Lord Lieutenant to the last newly appointed member of the Irish Constabulary, every Irishman loyal or disloyal, will know that the Bill will within a year or two become law and that Irish Nationalists will control the Parliament and the government of Ireland. Will not the House of Lords be urged by every alleged consideration of good sense and humanity to close without delay a period of uncertainty which is threatening to turn into a reign of anarchy or of terror? The question supplies its own answer. The second peril is one whereof nobody speaks, but which must occur to any man who has studied the history of the past eighteen years or reflects upon the condition of public opinion. The peril, to put the matter plainly, is that Home Rulers will not stop at attaining Home Rule for Ireland, and that they may, and probably will, attempt to undermine the political predominance of England. Everything points in this direction. The agitation for Home Rule has fostered in Ireland, and to a very limited extent in certain other parts of the United Kingdom, a feeling approaching to jealousy of English power. England or Great Britain is the predominant partner. England is wealthy, England is prosperous. England, as the language of common life imports, is the leading member of the United Kingdom. Lord Rosebery announced with wise foresight that Home Rule in Ireland could hardly be established with benefit to the United Kingdom until the assent thereto of the predominant partner had been obtained by force of argument. The idea was grounded on common sense. Will it not suggest to Irish Nationalists that their moment of authority must be used for obtaining far greater privileges for Ireland than the extravagant political power offered by Gladstonians in 1893? Is it not natural for Home Rulers to think that the predominant partner ought to be deprived of his predominance? The conduct of the Coalition and some of its leaders points in this direction. They will have obtained through the Parliament Act temporary, but strictly unlimited and dictatorial, power. They will have obtained it by intrigue; they have rejected and treated with scorn the idea of an appeal to the people. They have claimed, not for Parliament but for the existing House of Commons, an absolute legislative power superior to that of the nation, a power which I assert with confidence is not possessed by the elected Assemblies of the United States, or of the French Republic, or of the Swiss Confederation: And by a strange combination of circumstances one method for depriving the predominant partner of legitimate authority may seem to a Home Ruler to lie near at hand. Raise the cry of 'Home Rule all round,' or of 'Federalise the British Empire.' Turn England into one State of a great federation, let Wales be another, Scotland a third, the Channel Islands a fourth, and for aught I know the Isle of Man a fifth. Let the self-governing Colonies, and British India, send deputies to the Imperial or Federal Parliament. You may thus for a moment, under the pretence of uniting the Empire, not only divide the United Kingdom, but deprive England or Great Britain, in form at least, of that political supremacy and predominance which is the real bond of union and peace not only throughout the United Kingdom, but also throughout the length and breadth of the British Empire. I do not tremble for the power—the lawful and legitimate power—of England. Political devices, however crafty, break down whenever they are opposed to the nature of things. I know that unity is increasing throughout the Empire not through the cunning or the statecraft of politicians, but through the whole course of events. One part of our Imperial system becomes daily under the effect of railways, steamers, telegraphs, and the like, nearer and nearer to every other part. The sentiment of unity which is more valuable than any law aiming at formal federation each year gains strength. What I do fear and insist upon is the danger that a legislative dictatorship conferred on a party, and therefore necessarily taken away from the nation, should be employed in the attempt, vain though it ultimately must be, to deprive the predominant partner of a predominance requisite for the maintenance both of the United Kingdom and of the British Empire.

The four reflections at any rate which may be suggested by *A Leap in the Dark* are well worth the consideration of the loyal citizens of the United Kingdom.

A.V. Dicey.

Chapter I—Old And New Constitution

The Home Rule Bill<u>5</u> contains a New Constitution for the whole United Kingdom.<u>6</u>

The Bill bears on its face that its object is 'to amend the provision for the Government of Ireland'; it is entitled 'The Irish Government Act, 1893'; it is in popular language known as the Home Rule Bill. But all these descriptions are misleading. It is in truth a measure which affects the government alike of England, of Scotland, and of Ireland. It changes, to some extent the form, but to a far greater extent the working, and the spirit of all our institutions. It is a bold attempt to form a new constitution for the whole United Kingdom; it subverts the very bases of the existing constitution of England.

The present constitution of the United Kingdom is marked and has long been marked by two essential characteristics, the one positive and the other negative.

The positive characteristic is the absolute and effective authority of the Imperial Parliament throughout the length and breadth of the United Kingdom.

To this characteristic Englishmen are so accustomed that they hardly recognise its full importance. A government may make its power felt in three different ways—by the action of the Executive, including under that head all the agents of the Executive, such as the judiciary and the armed forces—by legislation—and by the levying of taxes. Take any of these tests of authority, and it will be found that the British Parliament is not only theoretically, but actually and effectively, supreme throughout the whole of Great Britain and Ireland. The Cabinet is virtually appointed by the Houses of Parliament; the army, the judges, the magistracy, all officials who throughout the country exercise executive power in any form whatever are directly or indirectly appointed by Parliament, and hold office subject to the will of Parliament. Of the legislative authority of Parliament as regards the United Kingdom it is scarcely necessary to speak. Any law affecting the United Kingdom not only lawfully may, but can in fact, be changed by the Imperial Parliament. Of the unlimited legislative authority ascribed to, and exercised by, Parliament in the United Kingdom the Home Rule Bill itself is sufficient evidence; and the Gladstonian Ministry, at any rate, see no reason why Parliament should not within the course of a few weeks remodel the fundamental laws of the realm. The right to impose taxes is historically the source of Parliamentary power, and in all matters of taxation Parliament has absolute freedom of action from one end of the United Kingdom to the other; whether the income tax is to be lowered, raised, or abolished, whether some new duty, such as the cart and wheel tax, shall be imposed, whether the United Kingdom shall maintain free trade, or return to protection, how taxes shall be raised and how they shall be spent—all matters in short connected with revenue are throughout the United Kingdom determined and determinable in the last resort by Parliament alone.

Hence, as things now stand, no kind of governmental action in any part of Great Britain and Ireland escapes Parliamentary supervision. The condition of the army, the management of the police, the misconduct of a judge, the release of a criminal, the omission to arrest a defaulting bankrupt, the pardon of a convicted dynamiter, the execution of a murderer, the interference of the police with a public meeting, or the neglect of the police to check a riot in London, in Skye, or in Tipperary, any matter, great or small, with which the executive is directly or indirectly concerned, is, if it takes place in any part of the United Kingdom, subject to stringent and incessant Parliamentary supervision, and may, at any moment, give rise to debates on which depend the fate of ministries and parties. If there be such a thing as supreme actual and effective authority, such authority is throughout the whole of the United Kingdom exercised by the Imperial Parliament, not occasionally and in theory, but every day and in the ordinary course of affairs.

This exertion of actual and effective power by the Imperial Parliament throughout the United Kingdom is a totally different thing from the supremacy or sovereignty exercised by Parliament throughout the whole British Empire. As a matter of legal theory Parliament has the right to legislate for any part of the Crown's dominions. Parliament may lawfully impose an income tax upon the inhabitants of New South Wales; it may lawfully abolish the constitution of the Canadian Dominion, just as some years ago it did actually abolish the ancient constitution of Jamaica. But though Parliament does in fact exert a certain, or rather a very uncertain, amount of power throughout the whole Empire, we all know that the Imperial Parliament neither exercises, nor claims to exercise, in a self-governing colony such as New Zealand,[7] that kind of effective authority which Parliament exercises in the United Kingdom. The Cabinet of New Zealand is not appointed at Westminster; the action of a New Zealand Ministry as regards the affairs of New Zealand is not controlled by the English Government. Not a pennyworth of taxation is imposed on the inhabitants of New Zealand, or of any colony whatever, by the Imperial Parliament. Even the imposition of customs, though it has an important bearing on the interest of the Empire, is in a self-governing colony determined by the colonial, and not by the British, Parliament. It is the Parliament of New Zealand, and not

9

the Parliament of England, which governs New Zealand. The Imperial Parliament, though for Imperial purposes it may retain an indefinite supremacy throughout the British Empire, has, as regards self-governing colonies, renounced, for all other than Imperial purposes, executive and legislative functions. To labour this point may savour of pedantry. But the distinction insisted upon, whilst often overlooked, is of extreme importance. We risk being deceived by words. The Imperial Parliament is supreme in the United Kingdom, it is also supreme in New Zealand. But the supremacy of the Imperial Parliament is a misleading expression; it means one thing in the United Kingdom, and another thing in New Zealand or in Canada. In the United Kingdom it means the exercise of real, actual, effective and absolute authority. In New Zealand it means little more than the claim to regulate matters of a distinctly and exclusively Imperial character. The distinction is vital. The essential feature of the English constitution is the actual and direct government of the whole United Kingdom by the Parliament at Westminster. No change could be more fundamental than a change which, in England, Scotland, or Ireland, reduced this actual authority to the ultimate or reserved sovereignty exercised, or rather claimed, by Parliament in Canada or in New Zealand.

The negative characteristic of the English constitution is the absence of federalism or of the federal spirit.

The spirit of institutions is as important as their form, and the spirit of English Parliamentary government has always been a spirit of unity.

The fundamental conditions of federal government are well known. They are first the existence of States such as the Cantons of Switzerland or the States of Germany, which are capable of bearing in the eyes of their inhabitants an impress of common nationality, and next the existence among the inhabitants of the federalised country of a very peculiar sentiment, which may be described as the desire for political union without the desire for political unity.[8] This condition of opinion leads to a division of powers between the federal or national government and the States. Whatever concerns the nation as a whole is placed under the control of the federal power. All matters which are not primarily of common interest remain in the hands of the States. Now each of these conditions upon which federalism rests has, as a matter of history, been absolutely unknown to the people of England. In uniting other countries to England they have instinctively aimed at an incorporate not at a federal union. This absence of the federal spirit is seen in two matters which may appear of subordinate, but are in reality of primary, consequence. Every member of Parliament has always stood on a perfect equality with his fellows; the representatives of a county or of a borough, English members, Scottish members, Irish members, have hitherto possessed precisely equal rights, and have been subject to precisely the same duties. They have been sent to Parliament by different places, but, when in Parliament, they have not been the delegates of special localities; they have not been English members, or Scottish members, or Irish members, they have been simply members of Parliament; their acknowledged duty has been to consult for the interest of the whole nation; it has not been their duty to safeguard the interests of particular localities or countries. Hence until quite recent years English parties have not been formed according to sectional divisions. There has never been such a thing as an English party or a Scottish party. Up to 1832 the Scottish members were almost without exception Tories; since 1832 they have been for the most part Liberals or Radicals; they have kept a sharp eye upon Scottish affairs, but they have never formed a Scottish party. The same thing has, to a great extent, held good of the Irish members. The notion of an Irish party is a novelty, and in so far as it has existed is foreign to the spirit of our institutions. Hence further, the Cabinet has been neither in form nor in spirit a federal executive. No Premier has attempted to constitute a Ministry in which a given proportion of Irishmen or Scotchmen should balance a certain proportion of Englishmen. English politicians have as yet hardly formed the conception of an English party. Not a single Prime Minister has claimed the confidence of the country on the ground that his colleagues were, or were not, English, Scottish, or Irish. That a Premier should glory in his pure Scottish descent is an innovation; it is an innovation ominous of revolution; it betrays a spirit of disintegration. If at the moment it flatters Scottish pride, Scotchmen and Irishmen would do well to recollect that it is a certain presage of a time when some Englishman will rise to power and obtain popular support on the ground of his staunch English sympathies and of his unadulterated English blood.

Now place the new constitution side by side with the old. Assume, as I do assume throughout this chapter, that our new Gladstonian policy works in accordance with the intentions of its authors.

The new constitution abolishes in Ireland the actual and effective control and authority of the Imperial Parliament.

The government of Ireland is under the Home Rule Bill[9] placed in the hands of an executive authority, or, in plain terms, a Cabinet, undoubtedly to be appointed by the Irish Legislature, in the same sense in which an English Cabinet is appointed by the British Parliament, or a New Zealand Cabinet is appointed by the Parliament of New Zealand.[10] For the first time in the whole course of history the administration of Irish affairs is placed in the hands of an Irish Ministry, in the selection of which the Imperial Parliament has no hand or concern whatever. Mr. McCarthy, Mr. Healy, Mr. Redmond,

Mr. Davitt, any leader, known or unknown, loyal or disloyal, who commands the confidence of the Irish Legislature, or, as I will venture to term it, the Irish Parliament,11 will naturally become the Premier of Ireland, and, together with his colleagues, will possess all the authority which belongs to a Parliamentary Executive. On the action of this Irish Cabinet the Bill places, with rare exceptions, either no restrictions at all or restrictions which are only transitory.12 Speaking generally, we may lay down that, except as to the control of the army, if that be an exception, the Irish Cabinet will, when the constitution gets into full working order, occupy in Ireland the position now occupied by the British Cabinet in regard to the whole United Kingdom. The appointment of officials, the conduct of Irish affairs, all the ordinary functions of government will, with certain exceptions meant for the most part to protect the rights of the Imperial Parliament, be exercised by Irish Ministers responsible to the Irish Parliament; and the British or Imperial Parliament will, in the ordinary course of things, have no more to do with the administration of affairs in Ireland than it has to do with the administration of affairs in New Zealand. The Irish, not the British, Cabinet will decide what are the steps to be taken for the protection throughout Ireland of the rights of property or of personal liberty; the Irish and not the English Cabinet will determine by what means the payment of rent is to be enforced; the Irish and not the English Cabinet will decide what persons are to be prosecuted for crime; the Irish and not the English Cabinet will determine whether the means for enforcing the punishment of crime are adequate, and whether Ireland, or some part of Ireland, say Belfast, requires to be governed by means of a Coercion Act; the Irish and not the English Cabinet will decide with what severity wrong-doers are to be punished, and whether, and under what circumstances, convicted criminals deserve either pardon or mitigation of punishment.

It is patent that under the new constitution the Irish Parliament and, under ordinary circumstances, the Irish Parliament alone will legislate for Ireland. For the Irish Parliament can, subject to certain Restrictions,13 pass any law whatever 'for the peace, order and good government of Ireland, in respect of matters exclusively relating to Ireland or some part thereof'14; and, subject to the same Restrictions, may repeal any law which, before the Home Rule Bill becomes law, is in force in Ireland. Under the new constitution the Irish Parliament and not the Imperial Parliament will, it is clear, as a rule legislate for Ireland. Under the new constitution the Irish Parliament may enact a Coercion Act, applying say to Ulster, or may repeal the existing Crimes Act. It may abolish trial by jury15 altogether, put any restraints it sees fit on the liberty of the press, or introduce a system of administrative law like that which exists in France, but is totally foreign to English notions of jurisprudence.

Under the new constitution, again, the financial relations of Great Britain and Ireland are made the subject of an elaborate arrangement which may fairly be called a contract16. Ireland takes over certain charges17, and speaking very generally, whilst all the duties of customs levied in Ireland are collected by and paid over to the Exchequer of the United Kingdom, as Ireland's contribution to Imperial expenditure, all the other taxes are, as a general rule, paid over to the Irish Exchequer. The justice or the policy of these financial arrangements is for my present purpose immaterial. All that need be observed is that the ordinary taxation of Ireland passes from the hands of the Imperial Parliament into the hands of the Irish Parliament, and that under the new constitution this arrangement is a settlement which the Imperial Parliament is morally bound to respect for a period of at least fifteen years18.

In Ireland therefore the new constitution abolishes the effective exercise of authority by the Imperial Parliament in matters of administration, in matters of legislation, in matters of finance; every concern which affects the daily life of Irishmen will be under the control of the Irish Cabinet and the Irish Parliament. The relation of the Imperial Parliament towards Ireland will not be the relation which it now occupies towards the whole United Kingdom, and which under the new constitution it will still occupy towards Great Britain. The Imperial Parliament, it is true, retains considerable reserved powers; what are the effect and nature of these powers shall be considered in its due place. The matter upon which I now insist is simply this: the new constitution does in any case transfer the effective government of Ireland from the Imperial Parliament to the Irish Parliament. The authority reserved to the Imperial Parliament may be termed supremacy, or sovereignty, or may be described by any other fine-sounding name which we are pleased to use, but the fact remains unaltered that, as long as the new constitution stands and works, the Imperial Parliament will not govern Ireland in the sense in which it governs England and Scotland, and that such authority as it exerts in Ireland will be analogous not to the power which it now exercises there, but to the influence which it possesses in Canada or in New Zealand.19

The new constitution is at bottom a federalist or semi-federalist constitution; it introduces into English institutions many of the forms of federalism and still more of its spirit.

The Parliament sitting at Westminster becomes for the first time a Federal Congress.

Of its members, 567 will represent Great Britain; 80 will represent Ireland. The exact numbers are for the present purpose insignificant. The serious matter is that the Imperial Parliament undergoes an essential change of character. The British members will have, or are intended to have, no concern with the government of Ireland. The Irish members ought to have nothing to do with the government of Great Britain. On Imperial subjects the Imperial Parliament, or, to call it by its proper name, the Federal Congress, votes as a whole; on Irish subjects it does not vote at all; on British topics its British members only vote. The British and the Irish members, in short, alike represent, though in a very clumsy fashion, the States of a Confederacy. Though the fact be artfully concealed, we have under the new constitution already, in germ at least, a British State and an Irish State, a British Parliament and an Irish Parliament, and a third body consisting of these two Parliaments, which is the Imperial or Federal Parliament.[20]

The different features of federalism make their appearance though under strange forms.

The constitution imposes Restrictions on the powers of the State Governments and of the Federal Government.

This appears unmistakably in the limitations placed upon the authority of the Irish Parliament.

These Restrictions, be they wise or unwise, politic or impolitic, are perfectly in keeping with the constitutional arrangements of a Federal Government, but are absolutely unknown to the theory and practice of English parliamentary government.

The powers of the Imperial Parliament, it may be said, are under the new constitution subject to no limitations. In words this assertion is true, in substance it is false. If the constitution works properly the Imperial Parliament will clearly be subject to the terms of the Government of Ireland Act, 1893, or, in other words, of the Federal Constitution. This subjection is not absolute; it is moral, not legal, still it exists. A breach of the federal compact will be no light matter.

The constitution again, as one would expect under a federal scheme, provides for the enforcement of the compact.

In the case of Ireland this is manifest. The royal veto,[21] the power of the Courts, and ultimately of the Privy Council, to pronounce on the constitutionality of any Irish Act, and treat it as void if it is in excess of the authority bestowed upon the Irish legislature, the provisions for the legal determination of constitutional questions,[22] the arrangements as to the payment of the Irish customs into the Imperial Exchequer, the special and very anomalous position of the Exchequer Judges, are all attempts, whatever be their worth, to restrain the Irish legislature and government, or in effect the Irish people, from the undue assertion of State rights.

Restraints again are placed on the unconstitutional action of the Imperial or Federal Parliament. They are less obvious, but at least as real and effectual as the safeguards against the breach of the constitution by the Irish government or legislature. They are all summed up in the presence of the Irish representatives at Westminster. The only legitimate reason, if legitimate reason there be, for their presence is the guardianship of Irish rights under the constitution. It is for them to see that these rights are held sacred. No diminution thereof can take place without either the assent of the Irish members or else the existence of such a majority in the Parliament at Westminster as may override the protests of Ireland.23 No doubt this is not an absolute security. But whoever considers the habits of English political life will conclude that, except in the event of the Imperial Parliament being resolved to suspend or destroy the constitution, there exists the highest improbability that any inroad should be made upon the privileges conferred under the new constitution upon Ireland. The security, though not absolute, is a good deal better than any safeguard given by the Bill that the State rights of Great Britain shall be duly respected by the representatives from Ireland. Assume, however, that the constitution works properly, and that all parties respect the spirit of its provisions. The result is that the new constitution forms a fundamental law, fixing the respective rights of Ireland, of Great Britain, of the Irish Parliament, and of the Imperial Parliament.24

The federal arrangements which, utterly unknown as they are to our institutions, form the foundation of the new constitution, are as nothing compared with the recognition and fostering of the federal spirit.

Great Britain and Ireland constitute for the first time in history a confederation. The difference or opposition of their interests receives legislative acknowledgment: each country is to possess in reality, though not in name, State rights; each must rely upon the constitution for the protection of these rights; each may suffer from the encroachments of the Imperial or central power. Ireland may complain that the Imperial Parliament by legislation, or the Privy Council by judicial interpretation, encroaches on her guaranteed rights. Great Britain may complain either that Irish members intermeddle in British affairs, and thus British rights are violated, or that the Privy Council so interprets the constitution that the prerogatives of the Central Government (which be it remembered must in practice be identified with the power of England) are unduly diminished. To imagine such complaints is not to assume that the constitution works badly. They are of necessity inherent in the federal system. There exists no federal government throughout the world where such complaints do not arise, and where they do not at times give rise to heart-burnings. It is well indeed, judging from the lessons of history, if they do not produce bitter conflicts, or even civil war. Let us take, however, the most sanguine view possible. Let us grant that both in England and in Ireland every minister, every legislator, every judge, is inspired with a spirit of perfect disinterestedness and absolute fairness. This concession, immense though it be, does not exclude vital differences of opinion. In our new confederacy, as in every other, there will arise the contest between State rights and federal rights, between the authority of the Central Government and of the State Government. In any case, a whole class of new difficulties and questions of a totally new description will make their appearance in the field of English politics, and call for the exercise on the part both of English and of Irish statesmen of extraordinary wisdom and extraordinary self-control. The new constitution in short, in virtue of its federal tendencies, will revolutionise the public life of the United Kingdom.

From whatever side the matter be considered we arrive at the same result. The Home Rule Bill is a new constitution; it subverts the bases of the English constitution as we now know it, for it destroys throughout Ireland the effective authority of the Imperial Parliament, and turns the United Kingdom into a federal government of a new and untried form.

The change may be necessary or needless, wise or unwise. The first and most pressing necessity of the moment is that every elector throughout the United Kingdom should, realise the immense import of the innovation. It is a revolution far more searching than would be the abolition of the House of Lords or the transformation of our constitutional monarchy into a presidential republic.

The next point to which the attention of every man throughout the land should be directed is, that the new constitution offered to us for acceptance is unknown to any other civilised country. Parts of it are borrowed from the United States; some of its provisions are imported from the British colonies, whilst others are apparently the inventions of the unknown and irresponsible Abbé Siéyès, who is the ingenious constitution-maker of the Cabinet. But the new polity as a whole resembles in its essence neither the American Commonwealth nor the Canadian Dominion, nor the Government either of New Zealand or of any other self-governing colony. It is an attempt—its admirers may think an original and ingenious attempt—to combine the sovereignty of an Imperial Parliament with the elaborate limitation and distribution of powers which distinguish federal government. The whole thing is an experiment and an experiment without precedent. Its novelty is not its necessary condemnation, but neither on the other hand is innovation of necessity the same thing as reform. The institutions of an ancient realm are not exactly the *corpus vile* on which theorists hard pressed by the practical difficulties of the political situation can be allowed to try unlimited experiments. We are bound to scrutinise with care every provision of this brand-new polity. We are bound to consider what will be their effect according to the known laws of human nature and under the actual circumstances of the time. It is vain to tell us that many of our institutions remain untouched. The introduction of new elements into an old political system may revolutionise the whole; the addition of new cloth to an old garment may, we all know, rend the whole asunder. There is no need for panic; there is the utmost need for prudence.

Chapter II—The New Constitution

A critic of the new constitution, intent on ascertaining how it affects the relation of Great Britain and Ireland, will do well to divert his attention from the numerous details of the Home Rule Bill, important as many of them are,[25] and fix his mind almost exclusively upon the four leading features of the measure.

These are:—

First. The supremacy of the Imperial Parliament.

Secondly. The retention of the Irish members in the Parliament at Westminster.

Thirdly. The powers of the Irish Government, in which term is here included both the Irish Executive and the Irish Parliament.

Fourthly. The Restrictions (popularly known as the safeguards) and the obligations imposed upon the Irish Government.

These features are primary and essential; everything else, however important in itself, is subsidiary and accidental.

A. *The Supremacy of the Imperial Parliament*[26]

The Home Rule Bill asserts in its preamble the inexpediency of 'impairing or restricting the supreme authority of Parliament'; and in clause 33, apparently[27] assumes the right of the Imperial Parliament after the passing of the Home Rule Bill to enact for Ireland laws which cannot be repealed by the Irish Parliament.

The new constitution therefore maintains the supremacy of the Imperial Parliament.

What, however, is the true meaning of this 'supreme authority,' 'supremacy,' or 'sovereignty,' if you like, of the Imperial Parliament?

The term, as already pointed out,[28] is distinctly ambiguous, and unless this ambiguity is cleared up, the effect of the Home Rule Bill, and the nature of our new constitution, will never be understood.

The supremacy of the Imperial Parliament may mean the right and power of Parliament to govern Ireland in the same sense in which it now governs England, that is, to exercise effective control over the whole administration of affairs in Ireland, and for this purpose, through the action of the English

Government, or, when necessary, by legislation, to direct, supervise and control the acts of every authority in Ireland, including the Irish Executive and the Irish Legislature. If this were the meaning of the expression, the Imperial Parliament would, after the passing of the Home Rule Bill, as before, be as truly supreme in Ireland as in England, in Scotland, in the Isle of Man, or in Jersey. The Irish Executive and the Irish Parliament would, of course, be bodies possessing large—and it might be very dangerous—delegated powers, but they would stand in the same relation to the Imperial Parliament as does the London County Council, which also possesses large delegated powers, which administers the affairs of a population as large as that of Scotland and which, very possibly, may receive from Parliament as time goes on larger and more extended authority than the Council now possesses. This is the sense which many Gladstonians, and some Unionists, attribute to the term 'supremacy of Parliament.' It is not the sense in which the expression 'supreme authority of Parliament' is used in the Home Rule Bill.

The supremacy of Parliament may bear quite another sense; it may mean that Parliament, whilst completely giving up the management of Irish affairs (subject of course to the Restrictions contained in the Home Rule Bill) to the Irish Executive and the Irish Legislature, retains in Ireland, as elsewhere throughout the Empire, reserved sovereignty, or the theoretical right (which exceptionally though rarely may be put into practice) of passing laws for Ireland and of course, among other laws, an Act modifying or repealing the terms of the Home Rule Bill itself. If this is the meaning of the expression 'supreme authority of Parliament,' the Imperial Parliament will, after the passing of the Home Rule Bill, stand in substance in the relation to Ireland which Parliament occupies towards any important self-governing colony, such as is the Canadian Dominion or New Zealand. The Irish Executive and the Irish Parliament will on this view constitute the real substantial government of Ireland, just as the Ministry and the Parliament of New Zealand constitute the real and substantial government of New Zealand. No doubt the Imperial Parliament will retain the theoretical right to legislate for Ireland, *e.g.* to pass an Irish Coercion Act, just as Parliament retains the theoretical right to legislate for New Zealand or Canada. So the Imperial Parliament has the legal right to repeal or override any law passed by the New Zealand Parliament, to tax the inhabitants of New Zealand, or finally, by the repeal of the New Zealand Constitution Act, 1852, 15 & 16 Vict. c. 72, to abolish the constitution of New Zealand altogether. But these things Parliament will not, and to speak truly cannot, do in New Zealand. The inhabitants of New Zealand possess as regards their internal affairs for practical purposes complete independence. They are governed from Wellington, they are not governed from Westminster. If in short the supremacy of Parliament means under the Home Rule Bill in Ireland what it means under 15 & 16 Vict. c. 72 in New Zealand, the inhabitants of Ireland will, when the Home Rule Bill passes into law, be governed from Dublin, they will not be governed from Westminster. Every Irish Home Ruler, be he Parnellite or Anti-Parnellite,[29] believes that the supremacy of Parliament is intended to mean in Ireland what it means in New Zealand, and the Irish Home Rulers are right. Any one will see that this is so who reflects on the meaning of the policy of Home Rule, who studies the authoritative utterances of Gladstonian leaders, such as Mr. Gladstone[30] himself, Mr. Asquith,[31] or Mr. Bryce.[32] Gladstonian statesmen wrap up their meaning in vague generalities; they insist, and in one sense with truth, that the sovereignty of Parliament is reserved. They do not wish to alarm their English followers. It is possible that they conceal even from themselves how completely the Imperial Ministry and Parliament surrender the practical government of Ireland into the hands of the Irish Parliament and its leaders. But for all this, their own language and the Bill itself prove that the supreme authority of Parliament is under the new constitution to be taken in its limited, and what for the sake of distinction we may call its 'colonial' sense. This is proved, if evidence were wanting, by the provision[33] that after fifteen years from the time when the Bill passes into law the financial relations between England and Ireland may be revised in pursuance of an Address to the Crown from the House of Commons or from the Irish legislative assembly. If the Imperial Parliament retains an effective or practically unlimited supremacy, the provision is futile and needless. What necessity is there for enacting that a sovereign Parliament, which institutes, may alter a scheme of taxation? But the provision is intelligible enough on one supposition, and on one supposition only. It is both intelligible and in place if Parliament gives up the real right of governing Ireland and occupies towards what is now a part of the United Kingdom the position, or something very like the position, which Parliament occupies towards a self-governing colony. It then embodies a compact between England and Ireland, and institutes a regular method for revising their financial relations. But this very compact proves that as regards Ireland the Imperial Parliament, if it reserves to itself ultimate sovereignty, has for practical purposes surrendered the reality of control.

There is no need to assert that this supremacy of the Imperial Parliament means nothing. The assertion would not be true. The reservation of sovereign authority means something, but it does not mean much. It does not mean the power or the right to govern Ireland; it means at most the legal and moral right to modify, or put an end to, the new constitution if ever it works badly.

The power, indeed, to abolish the constitution can neither be given nor taken away by Acts of Parliament, by the declarations of English statesmen, or the concessions of Irish leaders, whether authorised or not to pledge the Irish people. It is given to Great Britain, not by enactments, but by nature; it arises from the inherent capacity of a strong, a flourishing, a populous, and a wealthy country to control or coerce a neighbouring island which is poor, divided, and weak.34 This natural supremacy will, if the interests of Great Britain require it, be enforced by armies, by ironclads, by blockades, by hostile tariffs, by all the means through which national predominance can make itself felt. All reference to superior power is, in controversies between citizens, hateful to every man endowed with a sense of humanity or of justice. But in serious discussions facts must be faced, and if, for the sake of argument, I contrast, much against my will, the power of Great Britain with the weakness of Ireland, let it be remembered that the conception of a rivalry or conflict is forced upon Unionists by the mere proposal of Home Rule. As long as we remain a United Kingdom, there is no more need to think even of hypothetical or argumentative opposition between the resources or interest of England and of Ireland than there is to consider what in case of a contest may be the relative force of London and of the Orkneys.

What, then, the new constitution secures is not the power, but the legal right to abolish the new constitution. It is a right to carry through a fundamental change by lawful means. The Bill legalises revolution. This is well, for it is desirable that in a civilised State every change of institutions should be effected by constitutional methods. But should the circumstances ever arise under which Great Britain is resolved, in spite of the wishes of the Irish people or a large portion thereof, to abolish Home Rule and exercise the right of reserved sovereignty, there is no reason to expect that Irishmen who oppose British policy will admit that her use of sovereign power is morally justifiable. By force, or the threat of force, the controversy will, we must expect, in the last instance, be decided. However this may be, we must now realise what the supremacy of Parliament, at any rate to the Irish leaders who accept it, really means. It means nothing but the right of the Imperial Parliament of its own authority to repeal the Home Rule Bill and destroy the new constitution. The right may be worth having. But it is not the right to govern Ireland or to control the Irish Government; it is not a means of government at all: it is a method of constitutional revolution, or reaction.

Some critic will object that this supremacy of Parliament means to him a good deal more than the mere right to abolish the constitution. So be it. Let the objector then tell us in precise language what it does mean. If his reply is that the term is ambiguous, that its meaning must be construed in accordance with events, and may, according to circumstances, be restricted or extended, then he suggests that Parliamentary supremacy is not only an empty right, but an urgent peril. Nothing can be more dangerous than a compact between

England and Ireland which the contracting parties construe from the very beginning in different senses. If by asserting the supreme authority of Parliament English statesmen mean that Parliament reserves the right to supervise and control the government of Ireland, whilst Irishmen understand that Parliament retains nothing more than such a kind of supremacy or sovereignty as it asserts, rather than exercises, in New Zealand, then we are entering into a doubtful contract which lays the sure basis of a quarrel. We are deliberately preparing the ground for disappointment, for imputations of bad faith, for recriminations, for bitter animosity, it may be for civil war. If there be, as is certainly the case, a fair doubt as to what is meant by the supremacy of Parliament, let the doubt be cleared up. This is required by the dictates both of expediency and of honour. Meanwhile we may assume that the supremacy of Parliament, or the 'supreme authority of Parliament,' means in substance the kind of sovereignty which Parliament exercises, or claims to exercise, in every part of the British Empire.

For the maintenance of such supremacy, be it valuable or be it worthless, Great Britain pays a heavy price. For the sake of 'an outward and visible sign of Imperial supremacy' we retain eighty Irish members in the Imperial Parliament.35

B. The Retention of the Irish Members in the Imperial Parliament

This is now36 an essential, or at least a most important part of the ministerial policy for Ireland, yet it is a proposal which even its advocates must find difficult of defence. In 1886 every Gladstonian leader told us that it was desirable, politic, and just to exclude Irish members from the Parliament at Westminster; this exclusion was pressed upon England (plausibly enough) as a main advantage to be derived from the concession of Home Rule to Ireland. In 1893 every Gladstonian leader tells us that it is desirable, politic, and just to retain the Irish members at Westminster, and their presence is, for some reason not easy to explain, treated as removing every objection to the concession of Home Rule to Ireland. This astounding variation of opinion in the doctors of the State savours of empiricism, not to say quackery. A surgeon who tells a patient that he will not live unless his leg is amputated may be right, and may be worthy of trust; another surgeon who asserts that amputation is unnecessary may be right, and worthy of trust. But the surgeon who one moment insists that amputation is necessary to the preservation of his patient's life, and the next moment that it is unnecessary and may be fatal, is not the kind of adviser who inspires confidence in his wisdom.

Let the ingenuity of Gladstonians reconcile, as best it can, the doctrine of 1886 with the doctrine of 1893. To a man of sense who weighs the matter without reference to considerations of party, one thing will soon become apparent: the retention at Westminster of eighty, or indeed of any Irish members at all, means under a scheme of Home Rule the ruin of Ireland and the weakness of England.

As to Ireland.—The presence of Irish members at Westminster robs Ireland of the one advantage which Home Rule might by any possibility confer upon that country.

Any man in order to see that this is so has only to consider, first, what may under favourable circumstances be the benefit of Home Rule to Ireland, and next what is the natural result of summoning Irish members to the Parliament at Westminster.

The best conceivable result of Home Rule is that it may detach Irishmen from interest in English politics, and induce the most respected and respectable men in Ireland to take matters into their own hands and manage for themselves all strictly Irish affairs. For the last twenty years, at least, Ireland has been represented, or misrepresented, by eighty and more politicians, nominated in the main by Mr. Parnell. No one supposes for a moment that the Nationalist leaders who appeared before and were condemned by the Special Commission are fair samples of the Irish people. They are, take them at their best, reckless agitators. They were chosen by their patron, Mr. Parnell, not on account of their worth or talent, but because they were apt instruments for carrying out a policy of parliamentary intrigue, reinforced by a system of lawless oppression.[37] These men are the product of a revolutionary era; they no more represent the virtues and the genius of the Irish people than the demagogues or fanatics of the Jacobin Club represented the genius and the virtues of the French nation. We all know that Ireland abounds in citizens of a very different stamp. She has never lacked among her sons, and does not lack now, men of virtue, of vigour, and of genius. Throughout the length and breadth of the country you will find hundreds of men of merit—landlords whose lives have been honourable to themselves, and a blessing to their tenants; merchants as honest and successful as any in England or in Scotland; small landowners and tenant farmers who have paid their rent and paid their way, who have cultivated their land, who have never insulted or boycotted their neighbours, and have never been driven by intimidation into meanness and fraud. Add to these lawyers, thinkers, writers, and scholars, who rival or excel the best representatives of their class in other parts of the United Kingdom. These good men and true are not peculiar to any one creed or party; they are not confined to any one province, or to any one class; they are scattered through every part of the land; they are the true backbone of Ireland; they have saved her from utter ruin; they may still by their energy raise her to prosperity. But they have been thrust out of politics by the talkers, the adventurers, the conspirators. It is possible that if Home Rule compels Irishmen to turn their whole minds to Irish affairs, the so-called representatives who misrepresent their country may be dismissed from the world of politics, and the Parliament at Dublin be filled with members who, whether they come from the North or from the South, whether Unionists or Home Rulers, whether Roman Catholics or Protestants, whether landowners, tenant farmers, ministers of religion, merchants, or tradesmen, represent the real worth and strength of the country. If this should happen, Home Rule would still entail great evils on the whole United Kingdom. But even zealous Unionists might hope that for these evils Ireland at least will obtain some compensation. This hope, if the Irish members are retained at Westminster, will never be fulfilled.

For even the occasional presence38—which will in practice be the frequent presence—of the Irish members at Westminster destroys every hope that Ireland will be governed by her best citizens. The reasons why this is so are various; some of them may be shortly stated. The system, in the first place, of double representation, under which members of the Irish Parliament must flit to and fro between Ireland and England, and debate one day about Irish matters in Dublin, and the next about Imperial, or in truth British, matters in England, makes it impossible for quiet hard-working Irishmen, who carry on the real business of Ireland, to take part in politics. The political centre of interest, in the second place, will after, as before, the passing of the Home Rule Bill, be placed in London and not in Dublin. The humdrum local business which under a system of Home Rule ought to be discussed in the Irish Parliament, may vitally concern the prosperity of every inhabitant of Ireland, but it will not in general lend itself to oratory, or arouse popular excitement. The questions, on the other hand, to be discussed in the Imperial Parliament at Westminster, as, for example, whether Mr. Gladstone or Lord Salisbury shall be head of the British Cabinet, whether the royal veto on Irish legislation shall be exercised on the advice of the English or of the Irish Ministry, are matters which do not in reality greatly affect the happiness of ordinary Irishmen. But they give room for management, for diplomacy, for rhetoric, and are certain on occasions to arouse both the interest and the passions of the Irish people. We may take it for granted that the character of the Irish representation at Westminster will govern the character of the Parliament at Dublin.39 Hence arises a third and fatal obstacle to the active participation in Irish public life of Irishmen who are not professional politicians. The Home Rule Bill of 1893 professes to restrain on every side the action of the Irish government and Parliament. These Restrictions are the comfort of English Gladstonians; they are thought to be safeguards, though in reality there is nothing which they make safe. But Restrictions which delight Gladstonians are hateful to Irish Home Rulers. Their watchword is, 'Ireland a nation.' To this cry every Home Ruler will rally, and so too will, if once the Union is broken up, many an ardent loyalist, converted by anger at England's treachery into an extreme Nationalist. Irishmen will wish for an Irish army; they will wish for a protective policy; they will desire that Ireland shall play a part in foreign affairs, and will claim for her at least the independence of such a colony as New Zealand. To all these wishes, and to many more, some of which under a system of Home Rule are quite reasonable, the terms of the Home Rule Bill are opposed. Home Rulers, and probably enough the whole Irish people, will insist that the Bill, which will then have become an Act, must be modified. How is the modification to be obtained? How is Home Rule to be made a reality? By one method only: that is, by the freest use of those arts Of intrigue and obstruction by which Home Rule will have been gained. But for the carrying out of such a policy the agitators and intriguers who for the last twenty years have weakened and degraded the Imperial Parliament are the proper agents. For this work they, and they alone, are fit. The quiet, industrious, stay-at-home merchants or lawyers, who might be sent to Dublin for a month or two in the year to manage Irish business on business-like principles, will not be sent to Westminster to hold the balance between English parties. They cannot leave their every-day work; were they willing to forsake their own business, they are not the men to conduct with success the parliamentary game of brag, obstruction, and finesse. Keep, in short, the Irish members at Westminster, and you ensure the supremacy in Ireland of professional politicians. By a curious fatality the Gladstonian policy which weakens England ruins Ireland. Let no one fancy that this is the delusion of an English Unionist. Sir Gavan Duffy is an Irish Nationalist of a far higher type than the men who have drawn money from the Clan-na-Gael. In '48 he was a rebel, but if he was disloyal to England, he was always careful of the honour and character of Ireland. He, at least, perceives the danger to his country of retaining Irish members in a Parliament where they had ceased to have any proper place. 'For my own part,' he says, 'I should not care if they did not attend [the Imperial Parliament] for a generation, which will be needed for the manipulation of their own affairs.'

All this, I shall be told, is prophecy; Gladstonian hopes are as reasonable as Unionist fears. So be it. But in this matter my predictions have a special claim on the attention of the Ministry, they coincide with the forecast, or the foresight, of the present40 Chief Secretary for Ireland.

'Let us suppose that these Irish representatives for Imperial purposes are not chosen by the legislative body, but are chosen directly by Irish constituencies. You have already, according to our plan, two sets of constituencies. You have the 103 constituencies that return the popular branch of the legislative body, and you have those other constituencies up to seventy-five which return the elective members of the other branch of the legislative body. You have, therefore, got already on our plan two sets of constituencies. Now, if you are going to send members to Westminster for Imperial purposes to the number of forty-five or to the number of ninety-five, you must mark out a third set of constituencies—you must have a third set of elections. A system of that kind does not strike me at least as being exactly the thing for a country of which we are assured that before everything else its prime want is a profound respite from political turmoil. There are plenty of other objections from the Irish point of view, which I am not now going to dwell upon. Depend upon it that an Irish Legislature will not be up to the magnitude of the enormous business that is going to be cast upon it unless you leave all the brains that Irish public men have got to do Irish work in Ireland. Depend upon this, too, that if you have one set of Irish members in London it is a moral certainty that disturbing rivalries, disturbing intrigues would spring up, and that the natural and wholesome play of forces and parties and leaders in the Irish Assembly would be complicated and confused and thrown out of gear by the separate representatives of the country. All this is bad enough.'41

These are the words of my friend Mr. Morley.42 They were spoken at Newcastle on April 21, 1886. He was then, as now, responsible for the government of Ireland. Nothing can add to their gravity; nothing can add to their force; they were true in 1886, they remain as true to-day as they were seven years ago.43

As to England.—The presence of the Irish members at Westminster is on the face of it a gross and patent injustice to Great Britain. It is absurd, it is monstrous, that while the Irish Parliament and the Irish Parliament alone settle whether Mr. Healy, Mr. M'Carthy, Mr. Redmond, or Mr. Davitt is to be head of the Irish government, and England, though vitally interested in the character of the Irish Executive, is not to say a word in the matter, eighty Irishmen are to help in determining, and are often actually to determine, whether Lord Salisbury or Mr. Gladstone, Mr. Balfour or Mr. Chamberlain, is to be Prime Minister and direct the policy of England. Here again I can rely on the invaluable aid of Mr. Morley. He has denounced the effect on England of retaining Irish members at Westminster with a strength of language and a weight of authority to which it is impossible for me to make any pretension.

'But there is a word to be said about the effect on our own Parliament, and I think the effect of such an arrangement—and I cannot help thinking so till I hear of better arrangements—upon our own Parliament would be worse still. It is very easy to talk about reducing the number of the Irish members;

perhaps it would not be so easy to do. It is very easy to talk about letting them take part in some questions and not in others, but it will be very difficult when you come to draw the line in theory between the questions in which they shall take a part and those in which they shall not take a part. But I do not care what precautions you take; I do not care where you draw the line in theory; but you may depend upon it—I predict—that there is no power on the earth that can prevent the Irish members in such circumstances from being in the future Parliament what they were in the past, and what to some extent they are in the present, the arbiters and the masters of English policy, of English legislative business, and of the rise and fall of British Administrations. You will have weakened by the withdrawal of able men the Legislature of Dublin, and you will have demoralized the Legislature at Westminster. We know very well what that demoralisation means, for I beg you to mark attentively the use to which the Irish members would inevitably put their votes—inevitably and naturally. Those who make most of the retention of the Irish members at Westminster are also those who make most of there being what they call a real and effective and a freely and constantly exercised veto at Westminster upon the doings at Dublin. You see the position. A legislative body in Dublin passes a Bill. The idea is that that Bill is to lie upon the table of the two Houses of Parliament in London for forty days—forty days in the wilderness. What does that mean? It means this, that every question that had been fought out in Ireland would be fought out over again by the Irish members in our Parliament. It means that the House of Lords here would throw out pretty nearly every Bill that was passed at Dublin. What would be the result of that? You would have the present block of our business. You would have all the present irritation and exasperation. English work would not be done; Irish feeling would not be conciliated, but would be exasperated. The whole efforts of the Irish members would be devoted to throwing their weight—I do not blame them for this—first to one party and then to another until they had compelled the removal of these provoking barriers, restrictions, and limitations which ought never to have been set up. I cannot think, for my part I cannot see, how an arrangement of that sort promises well either for the condition of Ireland or for our Parliament. If anybody, in my opinion, were to move an amendment to our Bill in the House of Commons in such a direction as this, with all these consequences foreseen, I do not believe such an amendment would find twenty supporters.'44

This was the opinion of Mr. John Morley in 1886. A word in it here or there is inapplicable to the details of the present Bill; but in principle every syllable cited by me from his Newcastle address forms part of the Unionist argument against summoning as much as a single Irish member to Westminster. His language is admirable, it cannot be improved. All that any one who agrees with Mr. Morley can do in order to force his argument home is to point out in a summary manner the ways in which the Irish delegation at Westminster will enfeeble the Imperial Government.

First. The Irish members, or rather the Irish delegation, will have a voice and often a decisive voice in determining who are the men that shall constitute the English Cabinet; on the Irish vote will depend whether Conservatives, Liberals, Radicals, or Socialists shall administer the government of England. It is vain to tell us Irish members will be restrained, whether by law or custom, from voting on British affairs when they will vote on the most important of all British affairs, the composition and the character of the body which is to govern England.

That the Irish members will thus vote on a matter of special and vital importance to England is admitted. But things stand far worse than this. The vote of the Irish delegation will and must be swayed by an interest adverse to the welfare of Great Britain; for the interest of Great Britain, or, to use ordinary language of England, is that the English Government should be strong, and should represent the majority of the English or British electors. The direct interest of the Irish delegation is that the English Government should be weak, and represent the minority of English electors. That this is so is obvious. The weaker the British Government, the greater the weight of the Irish representatives. But if the English Cabinet represents a minority of the British people, and are kept in office only by the votes of their Irish allies, then the influence of the Irish representatives and the weakness of the English Government will have reached its extreme point. The effect therefore of the arrangement which brings Irish members to Westminster is to place the administration of English affairs in the hands of the party, whichever it be, that does not represent the wishes of the English people. This master stroke of Gladstonian astuteness ensures that Radicals shall be in office when the opinion of England is Conservative, and that Conservatives shall be in power when English opinion tends towards Radicalism.

Secondly. The retention of the Irish members breaks up our whole system of Cabinet government. This system has some inherent defects, but it cannot work at all with any benefit to the country unless the Cabinet can depend on the support of a permanent majority. The result of what has happily been described as the 'in-and-out plan,' that is the scheme for allowing Irish members to vote on some subjects and not on others, will be the constitution of two majorities, and it is more than possible that the one majority may belong to one party and the other majority to another. Look at the effect on the transaction of public affairs. The Irish members and the English Liberals combined may put in office a Liberal Cabinet. On English matters, *e.g.* the question of Disestablishment, or of Home Rule for Wales, the British majority consisting of British members of Parliament only may constantly defeat the Gladstonian Cabinet, and thus force into office a Conservative Cabinet which could command a majority on all subjects of purely British interest, but would always be in a minority on all matters of Imperial policy, *e.g.* on the conduct of foreign affairs. Which Cabinet would have a right to retain power? The sole answer is—neither. The proposed plan, in short, undermines our whole scheme of government.

Thirdly. The Irish members who are now simply Irish members of the Imperial Parliament will be transformed into a very different thing—an Irish delegation. The importance of this change cannot be over-rated. The essential merit of our present system of government is that the Executive, no less than the Parliament of the United Kingdom, represents the country as a whole. Our Premier may be a Scotsman, but we know of no such thing as a Scottish Premier. Englishmen may form the majority of the Cabinet, but we have never had an English Cabinet as contrasted with a Scottish or an Irish Cabinet. It has never been contended, hardly has it been hinted, that a Ministry ought to be made up of members taken in certain proportions from each division of the kingdom. But from the moment that sectional representation, and with it open advocacy of sectional interests, is introduced into the House of Commons, there will arise the necessity for the formation of sectional Cabinets.

The demand will be made, and the demand will be granted, that in the administration no less than in the House there shall be a system of representation; that England, that Scotland, that Ireland shall each have their due share in the Ministry. But this state of things must be fatal both to the capacity and to the fairness of the government. The talent of the Cabinet will be diminished, because the Prime Minister will no longer be able to choose as colleagues the ablest among his supporters without reference to the now irrelevant question whether they represent English, Scottish, or Irish constituencies. The character of the Executive will be lowered because the Cabinet itself will represent rival interests. It may seem that I am advocating the special claims of England. This is not so. I am arguing on behalf of the efficiency of the government of the United Kingdom. My argument is one to which Scotsmen and Irishmen should give special heed. If once we have cabinets and parties based upon sectional divisions, if we have English ministries and English parties as opposed to Scottish ministries or Irish ministries, and Scottish parties and Irish parties, it is not in the long run the most powerful and wealthy portion of what is now the United Kingdom which will suffer. It is hardly the interest of Scotsmen or Irishmen to pursue a policy which suggests the odious but inevitable cry 'England for

Englishmen.'

Fourthly, as long as Irish members remain at Westminster the English Parliament will never be freed from debates about Irish affairs.

This is a point there is no need to labour. Unless (what no honest man can openly propose) the 80 or 103 members from Ireland are to be taken from one Irish party only, they must represent different interests and different opinions. Some few at least will represent the wishes, the complaints, or the wrongs of Ulster. But if this be so, it is certain that the controversies which divide Ireland will make themselves heard at Westminster. Can any sane man fancy that if the Dublin Parliament passes an Act for the maintenance of order at Belfast, if the people of Belfast are suspected of intending to resist the Irish government, if Irish landlords, rightly or not, fear unfair treatment at the hands of the Irish Ministry or the Irish Parliament, none of these things will be heard of at Westminster? The supposition is incredible. Let Irish members sit at Westminster and Irish affairs will be debated at Westminster, and will often be debated when, under a system of Home Rule, it were much better they should be passed over in silence. Admit, what is not certain, that Home Rule in Ireland will occasionally withdraw a few Irish questions from discussion in England, it must be remembered that a new crop of Irish questions will arise. The federal character of the new constitution must produce in one form or another disputes and discussions as to the limits which bound the respective authority of the Imperial and of the Irish Governments. The Imperial Parliament will, for the first time, be harassed by the question of State rights. Add to this that at every great political crisis the House of Commons will have before it an inquiry which must produce interminable debates, namely whether a given bill is or is not a measure which concerns only the interest of Great Britain.

Two inducements are offered to England for the adoption of a plan the evils whereof were so patent in 1886 that it then could not, if we are to believe Mr. Morley,45 have commanded twenty supporters in the House of Commons.

The first inducement is that the presence of eighty Irish members at Westminster is an outward and visible sign of the supremacy of the Imperial Parliament.46 On this point it is needless to say much; few Englishmen will on consideration think it worth while to dislocate all our system of government in order that the British Parliament may retain in Ireland the kind of sovereignty which it retains in New Zealand. We are rightly proud of our connection with our colonies, but no one would seriously propose to retain nominal sovereignty in Canada at the price of a perilous and injurious change in the constitution of England.

The second inducement is that Great Britain will be allowed the exclusive management of British affairs.

This sort of spurious Home Rule for England turns out however to be as illusory a blessing as the maintenance of parliamentary supremacy.

Great Britain is, under the new constitution, not allowed to appoint the British Cabinet. Great Britain is forbidden to determine for herself any matter of legislation or administration which, however deeply it concerns British interests, trenches in the least degree on any Irish or Imperial interest. Any matter of finance, which comes within the wide head of Imperial liabilities, expenditure, and miscellaneous revenue,[47] falls within the competence of the Irish members. Questions of peace or war, our foreign relations, every diplomatic transaction, is a matter on which the Irish delegation may pronounce a decision. The conjecture is at least plausible[48] that Irish members will have a right to discuss and vote upon any subject debated in the Parliament at Westminster which involves the fate of a British Cabinet. Let it be granted that, if the provisions of the Home Rule Bill be observed, no Irish representative can vote 'on any Bill, or motion in relation thereto, the operation of which Bill or motion is confined to Great Britain.'[49] But then when is the operation of a Bill confined to Great Britain, or, to use popular language, what is a British Bill? This is an inquiry in the decision whereof the Irish members will take part. The Irish members, therefore, at Westminster will be judges of their own rights, and in the only cases in which it is of practical importance to Great Britain that the Irish representatives should not vote, will be able with the aid of a British minority to fix the limits of their own jurisdiction.[50] Let the Irish members and a British minority boldly vote that the operation of a Bill, say for the Disestablishment of the English Church, is not confined to Great Britain, and they can boldly vote that the Bill do pass, and no Court in Great Britain or the British Empire can question the validity of a law enacted in open defiance of the spirit or even the words of the Constitution.[51] The right of British members to the management of even exclusively British affairs will depend not upon the law of the land, but upon the moderation and sense of equity which may restrain the unfairness of partisanship.

For a parliamentary minority will, if only it throw scruples to the winds, be constantly able to transform itself into a majority by the unconstitutional admission of the Irish vote. This is not a power which any party, be it Conservative or Radical, English, Scottish, or Irish, ought to possess. Partisanship knows nothing of moderation. And the reason of this blindness to the claims of justice is that the spirit of party combines within itself some of the best and some of the worst of human passions. It often unites the self-sacrificing zealotry of religious fanaticism with the recklessness of the gambling table. Let an assailant of the Contagious Diseases Act, a fanatic for temperance, a protectionist who believes that free trade is the ruin of the country, an anti-vivisectionist who holds that any painful experiment on live animals is the most heinous of sins; let any man who has come to believe that his own credit, no less than the salvation of the country, depends on the success of a particular party, know that the triumph of his cause depends upon his voting that a particular measure operates beyond Great Britain, and we know well enough in which way he will vote. He will vote what he knows to be untrue rather than sacrifice a cause which he believes to be sacred. He will think himself both a fool and a traitor if he sacrifices the victory which is within his grasp to the maintenance of technical legality, or rather to respect for a rule of constitutional procedure.

Suppose, however, that I have underrated the equity of human nature, and that no faction in the House of Commons ever attempts to violate the spirit of the Constitution. The supposition is bold, not to say absurd; but even if its reasonableness be granted, this does not suffice for the protection of England's rights. The question whether a given Bill does or does not operate exclusively in Great Britain may often give rise to fair dispute, and (what should be noted) this dispute will always be decided against Great Britain in the only instances in which its decision is to Great Britain of any importance whatever. An example best shows my meaning. Let a Bill be brought forward for establishing Home Rule in Wales. Is the operation of the Bill confined to Great Britain? An English member, unless he is a Home Ruler, will answer with an undoubted affirmative. An English, or Irish, or Welsh Home Ruler will with equal certainty, and equal honesty, give a negative answer. The question admits of fair debate, but we know already how the debate will be decided. If the Unionists constitute a majority of the House, the Irish vote will be excluded. But in this case its exclusion is of no practical importance. If the Unionists constitute indeed a majority of British representatives, but do not constitute a majority of the House, the Irish vote will be included. The Irish representatives will decide whether Wales shall constitute a separate State, and the right of Great Britain to manage British affairs will not prevent the dismemberment of England. Home Rule, such as it is for England, means at best a totally different thing from Home Rule for Ireland. In the case of England it means a limited and precarious control of legislation for Great Britain by British members of Parliament. In the case of Ireland it means the real and substantial and exclusive government of Ireland by an Irish Ministry and an Irish Parliament.

But will the advantage of even this modified half-and-half Home Rule be really offered to England?

Gladstonians, it is rumoured (and before these pages are in print the rumour may turn out to be a fact), have their own remedy for some of the only too-patent absurdities of the 'in-and-out system' embodied in clause 9 of the Home Rule Bill. A suggestion is made which would be amusing for its irony, were it not revolting for its cynicism, that the difficulty of the double majority should be removed by the allowing members not only to remain at Westminster in their full number, but also to vote there on all matters whatever, including those affairs which exclusively concern the interests of Great Britain. This is no doubt a remedy for some of the evils of an unworkable proposal. It is a cure which to any Englishman of sense or spirit will seem tenfold worse than the disease. It is a cure in that sense only in which a traveller may be said to be relieved from the fear of robbery by a highwayman shooting him dead. The irregular interference of the Irish delegation in the formation of the British Cabinet, and other matters which indirectly concern England, is to be regularised (if I may use the term) by allowing to Irish members permanent despotism over England in matters which, on a system of Home Rule, concern England alone. Irish members may disestablish the Church of England, though England is to have no voice in the pettiest of Irish affairs. Irish members are to be allowed to impose taxes on England, say to double the income tax, though of these taxes no inhabitant of Ireland will pay a penny; the Irish delegation—and this is the worst grievance of all—is to be enabled, in combination with a British minority, to detach Wales from England, or to vote Home Rule for Scotland, or to federalise still further the United Kingdom by voting that Man, Jersey, and Guernsey shall send members to the Imperial Parliament. Note that all this may be done by the Irish delegation, though, under the new Constitution, England will not have a word to say on such questions as whether the right of electing members for the Parliament at Dublin shall or shall not be extended to every adult, or whether Ulster shall, or shall not, be allowed Home Rule of its own. The absurdity of this policy ought to prevent its ever being adopted; but in these days absurdity seems to tell as little against wild schemes of legislation as their injustice.

All this consideration of haggling and trafficking between Great Britain and Ireland is loathsome to every true Unionist who considers Englishmen and Irishmen as still citizens of one nation. But, when Gladstonians propose to divide the United Kingdom into two States, it is as essential as it is painful to weigh well what is the gain of Great Britain in the new scheme of political partnership. If the matter be looked at from this point of view, it is easy to see how miserable are the offers tendered to England. Compare for a moment the authority to be given her under the new constitution with the authority she has hitherto possessed or the authority tendered to her under the Home Rule Bill of 1886.

Up to 1782 the British Parliament held in its own hands the absolute control not only of every British affair, but every matter of policy affecting either Ireland or the British Empire. The British Parliament, in which sat not a single representative of any Irish county or borough, appointed the Irish Executive. The British Parliament, whenever it thought fit, legislated for Ireland; the British Parliament controlled the whole course of Irish legislation; every Act which passed the Parliament of Ireland was inspected, amended, and, if the English Ministry saw fit, vetoed in England. The system was a bad system and an unjust system. It is well that it ended. But as regarded the control of the British Empire it corresponded roughly with facts. The Empire was in the main the outcome of British energy and British strength, and the British Empire was governed by Great Britain.

The constitution of 1782 gave legislative independence to Ireland, but did not degrade the British Parliament to the position which will be occupied by the Imperial Parliament under the constitution of 1893. The British Parliament remained supreme in Great Britain; the British Parliament controlled the Imperial policy both of England and of Ireland. The British Parliament, or rather the British Ministry, virtually appointed the Irish Executive. The British Parliament renounced all rights to legislate for Ireland52; the British Parliament technically possessed no representatives in the Parliament at Dublin. But any one who judges of institutions not by words but by facts will perceive that in one way or another the influence and the wishes of the British Government were represented more than sufficiently in the Irish Houses of Parliament. Grattan's constitution, in short, left the British Parliament absolutely supreme in all British and Imperial affairs, and gave to the British Ministry predominating weight in the government of Ireland. This is a very different thing from the shadowy sovereignty which the English Parliament retains, but abstains from exercising, in our self-governing colonies. It is a very different thing from the nominal power to legislate for Ireland which the new constitution confers upon the Imperial Parliament.

Since the Union England and Ireland have been politically one nation. The Imperial or British Government has controlled, and the Imperial Parliament has passed laws for, the whole country. Nor has the presence of the Irish members till recent days substantially limited the authority of Great Britain. Till 1829 the Protestant landlords of Ireland who were represented in the Imperial Parliament shared the principles or the prejudices of English landowners. Since the granting of Catholic emancipation Roman Catholic or Irish ideas or interests have undoubtedly perplexed or encumbered the working of British politics. But the representatives of Ireland have been for the most part divided between the two great English parties, and it was not till Mr. Parnell's influence united the majority of Irish representatives into a party hostile to Great Britain that any essential evil or inconvenience resulted from their presence at Westminster. This inconvenience, whatever its extent, has been the price of the Union. The gain has been worth the payment: the action of Parliament has been hampered, but its essential and effective authority throughout the realm has been maintained.

In 1886 Mr. Gladstone framed a constitution which was meant to be a final and a just settlement of the questions at issue between England and Ireland. Under the constitution of 1886 Great Britain surrendered to Ireland about the same amount of independence as is offered her under the proposed constitution of 1893. But the difference in the position of Great Britain under the two constitutions is immense.

Under the constitution of 1886 Great Britain was offered a position of the highest authority.

To the British Parliament (in which was to sit not a single Irish member) was to fall the appointment of the British or Imperial Ministry. The British Parliament received absolute control of all British, colonial, Imperial, and foreign affairs. Perfect unity was restored to the spirit of her government, and predominance in the British, or, to use ordinary language, in the English, Parliament was given to the conservative elements of English society. Great Britain became mistress in her own home; she became much more than this; she was enthroned as undisputed sovereign of the British Empire.53

Under the constitution, in short, of 1886, if Great Britain was weakened on one side she was strengthened on another. Her Parliament obtained an immense accession of authority, and was all but entirely freed both from the necessity for considering Irish questions and from the damage of Irish obstruction. Ireland surrendered to England all share in the government of the Empire, and the further dismemberment of Great Britain without the assent of the British people became difficult, if not impossible. It does not lie in the mouth of Gladstonians to say that the measure of 1886 was unjust. It was laid before the country as a compromise which was just to England and to Ireland. The Irish leaders, we were told, accepted the proposal, just as we are told that they accept the proposed constitution of 1893. If the acceptance was honest, then in 1886 they agreed to a bargain far more favourable to England than the contract now pressed on our acceptance. If their acquiescence was a mere pretence, what trust can we place in the assertion that they accept the arrangement of 1893?

However this may be, it is clear that England is now offered a position of weakness and of inferiority such as she has never occupied during the whole course of her history. What is the meaning or justification of the proposed surrender by England of every compensation for Irish Home Rule which was offered her in 1886?

For this surrender Gladstonians assign but two reasons.

The presence of the Irish members at Westminster is, it is said, a concession to the wishes of Unionists.

This plea, even were it supported by the facts of the case, would be futile. It might pass muster with disputants in search of a verbal triumph, but to any man seriously concerned for the welfare of the nation must appear childishly irrelevant. The welfare of the State cannot turn upon the neatness of a *tu quoque*; retorts are not reasons, and had every Unionist, down from the Duke of Devonshire to the present writer, pressed in 1886 for the retention of the Irish members at Westminster, the controversial inexpertness of the Unionists seven years ago would not diminish the dangers with which, under a system of Home Rule, the presence of the Irish members at Westminster actually threatens England. But the plea, futile as it is, is not supported by fact. It rests on a misrepresentation of the Unionist position in 1886.

'The case in truth stands thus:—Mr. Gladstone was [in 1886] placed in effect in this dilemma: "If you do not," said his opponents, "retain the Irish representatives at Westminster, the sovereignty of the British Parliament will be, under the terms of your Bill, no more than a name; if you do retain them, Great Britain will lose the only material advantage offered her in exchange for the local independence of Ireland." Gladstonians, in substance, replied that the devices embodied in the Government of Ireland Bill at once freed the British Parliament from the presence of the Parnellites and safeguarded the sovereignty of the British, or (for in this matter there was some confusion) of the Imperial Parliament. On the latter point issue was joined. The other horn of the dilemma fell out of sight, and some Unionists, rightly believing that the Bill as it stood did not preserve the supremacy of the British Parliament, pressed the Ministry hard with all the difficulties involved in the removal of the Irish members. In the heat of debate speeches were, I doubt not, delivered in which the argument that you could not, as the Bill stood, remove the Irish members from Westminster and keep the British Parliament supreme in Ireland, was driven so far as to sound like an argument in favour of, at all costs, allowing members from Ireland to sit in the English Parliament. Those who appeared to fall into this error were, it must be noted, but a fraction of the Unionist Party, and their mistake was little more than verbal. When the Ministry maintained that the removal of the Irish members from Westminster was a main feature of their Home Rule policy, opponents naturally insisted upon the defects of the scheme laid before them, and did not insist on the equal or greater defects of a plan which the Government did not advocate. Mr. Gladstone, we are now told, has changed his position, and assents to the principle that Ireland must be represented in the British Parliament. If this assent be represented as a concession to the demands of Unionists, my reply is that it is no such thing. It is merely the acceptance of a different horn of an argumentative dilemma. Grant for the sake of argument (what is by no means certain) that the supremacy of the Imperial Parliament is really saved. The advantage offered to England in exchange for Home Rule is assuredly gone. My friend, Mr. John Morley, used to argue in favour of Home Rule from the necessity of freeing the English Parliament from Parnellite obstruction. As a matter of curiosity, I should like to know what he thinks of a concession which strikes his strongest argumentative weapon out of his hands. My curiosity will be satisfied on the same day which tells us Lord Spencer's reflections on the surrender of the policy represented by the Land Purchase Bill. Meanwhile, I know well enough the thoughts of every Unionist who is not tied by the exigencies of his political antecedents or utterances. To say that in the eyes of such a man the proposed concession is worthless, is to say far too little. It is not a concession which he rates at a low price; it is a proposal which he heart and soul condemns.'54

These words were not written to meet the present condition of the controversy; they were published in 1887 at a time when no Gladstonian, except Mr. Gladstone (if indeed he were an exception), knew whether the retention in the Parliament at Westminster, or the exclusion from the Parliament at Westminster, of the Irish members, was an essential principle of Home Rule.

England again, it is alleged, suffers without murmuring all the inconvenience caused by the Irish vote at Westminster; and she may well, under a system of Home Rule, bear without complaint evils which she has tolerated for near a century.

The answer to this reasoning is plain. It is a sorry plea indeed for a desperate innovation that it leaves the evils of the existing state of things no worse than they now are. For the sake of the maintenance of the Union, which Unionists hold of inestimable value, England has borne the inconvenience caused to her by the Irish vote. It argues simplicity, or impudence, to urge that England should continue to bear the inconvenience when the national unity is sacrificed for the sake of which it was endured. But the reply does not stop here. The presence of Irish members at Westminster under the new constitution increases and stereotypes the evils, whatever their extent, now resulting from the existence of 103 Irish members in the House of Commons. The evils are increased because the Irish members are turned into a delegation from the Irish State, and their action ceases to be influenced, as it now is, by the consideration—a very important one—that the Imperial Parliament not only in theory but in fact legislates for Ireland, and that the English Cabinet controls the Irish administration and directs the course of political promotion in Ireland. The sentiment and the interest of the Irish members will be changed. Whether they come from North or South they will be representatives of Ireland, and will naturally and rightly consider themselves agents bound in every case to make the best bargain they can for Ireland as against the United Kingdom, or, in plain language, as against England. They will no longer feel it their interest to keep in power the English party which they think will best govern Ireland, for with the government of Ireland the Imperial Parliament will, as long as the new constitution stands, have no practical concern. No honest Home Ruler supposes that, if the Home Rule Bill passes into law, the Imperial Parliament will, even should the tragedy of the Phoenix Park be repeated in some more terrible form, pass a Crimes Act for Ireland; to the Irish Government will belong the punishment of Irish crime. No interest will therefore restrain the Irish delegation from swaying backwards and forwards between the two English parties, in order to obtain from the one or the other some momentary advantage, or some lucrative concession, to the Irish people. Intrigue will be pardonable, diplomatic finesse will become a duty. This evil no doubt in some degree exists, but under the present state of things it admits of diminution. A just redistribution of the franchise will undoubtedly lessen the number of Ireland's representatives, whilst it will increase the relative importance, if not the actual numbers, of loyalists in the representation of Ireland. The gradual settlement of the land question, as Unionists believe, will further strike at the true root of Irish discontent, and in removing the true grievance of the Irish tenants will diminish the strength of the party which depends for its power on the revolutionary elements in Irish society. But all chance of mitigating the inconvenience inflicted upon England by the presence of the Irish members vanishes for ever when they are changed into an Irish delegation, and are compelled by their position to be the mere mouthpiece of Ireland's claims against England.

The alleged reasons for the weakening of England are untenable, and, were they tenfold stronger than they are, could not remove the flagrant contradiction between the Gladstonian policy of 1886 and the Gladstonian policy of 1893.

But a contradiction which cannot be removed may be explained.

The withdrawal of the Irish members from Westminster might give Ireland the chance of obtaining some of the benefits, and compensate England for some of the evils, of Home Rule. But however this may be, one result it would produce with certainty; it would dash the Gladstonian party to pieces. The friends of Disestablishment, the Welsh, or the Scottish, Home Rulers, the London Socialists, all the revolutionists throughout the country, know that with the departure of the Irish representatives from Westminster their own hopes of triumph must be indefinitely postponed. England is the stronghold of British conservatism, and an arrangement which leaves the fate of England in the hands of Englishmen may be favourable to reform, but is fatal to revolution. Has this fact arrested the attention of Gladstonians? I know not. It is an unfortunate coincidence that the least defensible portion of an indefensible policy should, while it threatens ruin to England, offer temporary salvation to the party who rally round Mr. Gladstone.55

C. The Powers of the Irish Government

I. *The Irish Executive.*

At the head of the Irish Executive will nominally stand the Lord Lieutenant; he will however in reality occupy the position of a colonial Governor, and be, for most purposes, little more than the ornamental figure-head of the Irish Administration. The real executive government of Ireland56 must be a parliamentary Ministry or Cabinet57 chosen in effect, though not in name, by the Irish Parliament, or rather by the Irish Legislative Assembly, or House of Commons, just as the English Cabinet is appointed in effect by the English House of Commons. Allowing then for the occasional intervention of the Lord Lieutenant as the representative of the Imperial Parliament to protect either the interests of the Empire or the special rights of the United Kingdom,58 the Irish Ministry is to occupy in Ireland the position which the New Zealand Ministry occupies in New Zealand, and will for most purposes as truly govern Ireland as the New Zealand Ministry governs New Zealand, or as Mr. Gladstone's Ministry governs England. The Irish Ministry will be the true Government of Ireland.

This is a fact to which the attention of the English public ought to be sedulously directed. The creation of an independent Irish Parliament strikes the imagination; it is seen to be an innovation of primary importance. The creation of an independent Irish Cabinet or Ministry is taken as a matter of course, and neither Unionists nor Gladstonians see its full import. Yet in Ireland, as elsewhere, the character of the Executive is of more practical consequence than the character of the Legislature. A country may dispense, for a long time, with legislation; no country can dispense with good government.

This principle holds good even in an orderly country such as England, where the sphere of the administration is far less extended than it is in most States. We might get on for a good while prosperously enough without a Parliament, or without new laws, but if anything deprived us even for a week of an Executive, or if, for any reason, the whole spirit of the public administration were changed, every Englishman would feel this portentous revolution in every concern of his daily life. The protection of the Government, of the army, of the police, of the law courts, are with us so much matters of course, that we never realise how much the comfort and prosperity of our existence hang upon it, nor do we reflect that the aid we derive from the Courts is in the last instance dependent upon the decisions of the judges being actively supported by the forces at the command of the executive power. Again, we are so used to the preservation on the part of the Executive and the Courts of an attitude of perfect impartiality and to the extension of their aid to all citizens alike, that we can hardly even in imagination conceive what would be the condition of things if the public administration favoured particular classes and looked askance on the rights of one class, whilst it enforced with rigour the rights of another. Yet events which have been passing before our eyes may show any one how absolutely dependent we may be, at any moment, for our enjoyment of life, property, or freedom upon the authority and the equity of the Executive. Consider the strike at Hull. Practically the legal rights and personal freedom of every inhabitant of the city depend upon the action of the Government. It is as plain as day that if the Government had taken actively and unfairly the side of one party or the other to the contest, the party which the Government favoured would at once have won. Suppose, though the supposition is a very improbable one, that the Home Secretary had directed the police to put down every form of picketing and to arrest every one who counselled the free labourers to desert their employment, the strike would come at once to an end. Suppose on the other hand—the supposition is also a wild one—that the Home Secretary had declined to protect the rights of the free labourers, that the troops had been withdrawn, and that the police had been inactive; suppose, in short, that the Government had been careless to maintain order. The Trade Unionists would at once have become supreme, and freedom of contract, as well as liberty of person, would have been at once abolished. Even in England then the power to exercise our rights as citizens has its source in the constant, though unobserved, intervention of the executive power. What is true of England is truer still of countries where the sphere of the administration is more widely extended than with us, and what is true of every civilised country is truest of all of Ireland. Ireland is a country where the sphere of the administration is large, and where it will probably be increased. Ireland is divided by hostile factions not too much prone to respect the law. Even as things stand, the Irish Executive finds it hard enough to hold a perfectly even and level course, and the whole state of the country depends upon the spirit in which the law is enforced. One of the very gravest defects of our present system is that in Ireland a change of government means, to a certain extent, a change in the administration of the law. Yet both Mr. Balfour and Mr. Morley have enforced the law, and have meant, according to their lights, to act towards all citizens with equitable impartiality. And Mr. Balfour, Mr. Morley, or any statesman appointed by the Imperial Parliament, is likely to act with more fairness than at the present moment would any Executive chosen by any Irish Parliament. One thing, at any rate, is certain. An independent Irish Executive will possess immense power. It will be able by mere administrative action or inaction, without passing a single law which infringes any Restriction to be imposed by the Irish Government Act, 1893, to effect a revolution. Let us consider for a moment a few of the things which the Irish Cabinet might do if it chose. It might confine all political, administrative, or judicial appointments to Nationalists, and thus exclude Loyalists from all positions of public trust. It might place the Bench,59 the magistracy, the police wholly in the hands of Catholics; it might, by encouragement f athletic clubs where the Catholic population were trained to the use of arms, combined with the rigorous suppression of every Protestant association suspected, rightly or not, of preparing resistance to the Parliament at Dublin, bring about the arming of Catholic and the disarming of Protestant Ireland, and, at the same time, raise a force as formidable to England as an openly enrolled Irish army. But the mere inaction of the Executive might in many spheres produce greater results than active unfairness. The refusal of the police for the enforcement of evictions would abolish rent throughout the country. And the same result might be attained by a more moderate course. Irish Ministers might in practice draw a distinction between 'good' landlords and 'bad' landlords, and might grant the aid of the police for the collection of reasonable, though refusing it for the collection of excessive rents, and might at last magnanimously recognise the virtues of Mr. Smith-Barry, whilst passing a practical sentence of outlawry on Lord Clanricarde. Is there anything absurd or unreasonable in the supposition that a Ministry of Land Leaguers chosen by a Parliament of Nationalists should attempt to enforce the unwritten law of the Land League? A Gladstonian who answers this question in the affirmative entertains a far lower opinion than can any candid Unionist of Mr. Gladstone's Irish allies. It would be the grossest unfairness to suggest that every man convicted of conspiracy by the Special Commission added to criminality and recklessness a monstrous form of hypocrisy, and that, whilst urging Irish peasants to boycott evictors and land-grabbers, he felt no genuine moral abhorrence of evictions and land-grabbing. But if, as is certainly the case, the founders of the Land League really detested the existing system of land tenure, and considered a landlord who exacted rent a criminal, and a tenant who paid it a caitiff, it is as certain as anything can be that they will be under the greatest temptation, not to say, in their own eyes, under a stringent moral obligation, to strain the power of an Irish Executive for the purpose of abolishing the payment of rent. Nothing, at any rate, will seem to an Irish Ministry more desirable than that within three years60 from the passing of the Bill landlords and tenants should come to an arrangement, and nothing is more likely to produce this result than the withdrawal from the landlords of the aid, if not the protection, of the law. My argument, however, at the present point does not require the assertion or the belief that an Irish Ministry will be guilty of every act of oppression which it can legally commit. All that I insist upon is that an Irish Ministry will exercise immense power, and that without violating a letter of the constitution, and without passing a single act which any Court whatever could treat as void, the Ministry will be able to change the social condition of Ireland. The Irish Cabinet, remember, will not be checked by any Irish House of Commons, for it will represent the majority of that House. It will not need to fear the interposition of the Imperial Ministry or the Imperial Parliament, for if the authorities in England are to supervise and correct the conduct of the Irish Cabinet, Home Rule is at an end. Mr. Asquith has repudiated all idea of creating two Executives in Ireland61 for the ordinary purposes of government, and from his own point of view he is right. The notion of a dual control is preposterous; the attempt to carry it out must involve anarchy or revolution. The Irish Ministry must in ordinary matters be at least as free as the Ministry of a self-governing colony. The independence of the Irish Executive is indeed a totally new phenomenon in Irish history, and is, as I have said, a far more important matter than the independence of the Irish Parliament, but it is an essential feature of Home Rule, and every elector throughout England should try to realise its import.

One check, indeed, is placed upon the power of the Irish Cabinet. The military forces of the Crown, and the Royal Irish Constabulary and Dublin Metropolitan Police (as long as they exist62), are subject to the control of the Imperial or English Ministry.63 The result is that the English Cabinet will have the means of using force in Ireland for the maintenance of order, for the execution of the law, or for the maintenance of the authority of the Imperial Parliament. But this advantage is after all purchased at the price of placing the country under the rule of something very like two Executives. If the policy of the Irish Cabinet, *e.g.* as to suppressing a riot at Dublin or Belfast, should differ from the policy of the English Cabinet, the ordinary police may be called into action whilst the army or the royal constabulary stand by inactive, or the army may disperse a meeting which the Irish Ministry hold to be a lawful assembly.

II. The Irish Parliament.

The authority of the Irish Parliament, whilst acting within the limits of the constitution, is extremely wide.64

The Parliament appoints the Irish Government of the day; it will determine whether Mr. M'Carthy or Mr. Redmond, Mr. Healy or Mr. Davitt, directs the Irish Administration. In this matter the British Government will have no voice. The English Ministry are under the new constitution expected in many ways to co-operate with the Irish Ministry, yet it is quite conceivable that the Ministers of the Crown at Dublin may be men whose whole ideas of expediency, of policy, of political morality, may be opposed to the ideas of the

Ministers of the Crown at Westminster.

The Irish Parliament, again, even if every Restriction on its powers inserted in the Home Rule Bill should pass into law, will be found to have ample scope for legislative action.65

It can repeal66 any Act affecting Ireland which was enacted before the passing of the Home Rule Bill. Thus it can do away with the right to the writ of *habeas corpus*; it can abolish the whole system of trial by jury; it can by wide rules as to the change of venue expose any inhabitant of Belfast, charged with any offence against the Irish Government, to the certainty of being tried in Dublin or in Cork. If an Irish law cannot touch the law of treason or of treason-felony, the leaders of the Irish Parliament may easily invent new offences not called by these names, and the Parliament may impose severe penalties on any one who attempts by act or by speech to bring the Irish Government into contempt. A new law of sacrilege may be passed which would make criticism of the Irish priesthood, or attacks on the Roman Catholic religion, or the public advocacy of Protestantism, practically impossible. The Irish House of Commons may take the decision of election petitions into its own hands, and members nominated by the priests may determine the proper limits of spiritual influence. Thus the party dominant at Dublin can, if they see fit, abolish all freedom of election; nor is this all that the Irish Parliament can accomplish in the way of ensuring the supremacy of an Irish party. After six years from the passing of the Home Rule Bill—let us say in the year 1900—the Irish Parliament can alter the qualification of the electors and the distribution of the members among the constituencies. Parliament can in fact introduce at once universal suffrage, and do everything which the ingenuity of partisanship can suggest for diminishing the representation of property and of Protestantism. If, further, in any part of Ireland there be reason to fear opposition to the laws of the Irish Parliament, a severer Coercion Act may be passed than any which has as yet found its way on to the pages of the English or the Irish Statute Book. Worse than all this, the Irish Parliament has the right to legislate with regard to transactions which have taken place before the passing of the Home Rule Bill. An Act inflicting penalties on magistrates who have been zealous in the enforcement of the Crimes Act, an Act abolishing the right to recover debts incurred before 1893, an Act for compensation to tenants who had suffered from obedience to the behests of the Land League, are all Acts which, however monstrous, the Irish Parliament is, under the new constitution, competent to pass.

My assertion is, be it noted, not that all or any of such laws would be passed, but that the passing of them would, under the new constitution, be legal. The Irish Parliament could further by its legislation pursue lines of policy opposed to the moral feeling and political judgment of Great Britain, and this too where Irish legislation practically affects Great Britain. State lotteries might be re-established, gambling tables might be re-opened at Dublin. If the imposition of protective duties on imported goods is forbidden, there is nothing apparently to prevent the reintroduction of Protection into Ireland by the payment of bounties; there is certainly nothing to prohibit the repeal or suspension of the Factory Acts, so that English manufacturers might be compelled to compete with Irish rivals who are freed from the limits imposed upon excessive labour by the humanity or the wisdom of England. The power of the Irish Parliament to pass laws which in the eyes of Englishmen are unwise or inequitable, is, it will be urged, an essential part of the policy of Home Rule. I admit that this is so. But this makes it the more necessary that English electors should realise what this essential characteristic of Home Rule means, or may mean. The Nonconformist conscience exposed Irish Home Rulers to painful humiliation and possible ruin by forbidding them to follow the political leader of their choice to whom they had deliberately renewed their allegiance. Is it certain that Englishmen who could not tolerate the official authority of Mr. Parnell will bear the official leadership, say of Mr. Healy, if employed to carry out the economical principles of Mr. Davitt?

The legislative powers, ample as they are, of the Irish Parliament are in some respects restricted, but what the Parliament cannot accomplish by law it could accomplish by resolution. The expressed opinion of a legislature entitled to speak in the name of the people of Ireland must always command attention, and may exert decisive influence. Suppose that the Irish House of Commons asserts in respectful, but firm, language, the right of the Irish people to establish a protective tariff; suppose that when England is engaged in a diplomatic, or an armed, contest with France, the Irish House of Commons resolves that Ireland sympathises with France, that Ireland disapproves of all alliance with Germany, that she has no interest in war, and wishes to stand neutral; or suppose that, taking another line, the Irish Parliament at the approach of hostilities resolves that the people of Ireland assert their inherent right to arm volunteers, or raise an army in their own defence. No English Minister can allege with truth that these resolutions or a score more of the same kind are a breach of the constitution; yet such resolutions will not be without their effect in England; they cannot be without their effect abroad; in many parts of Ireland they will have more than the authority of an Act of Parliament.

Assume, for the purpose of my argument, that the Irish Parliament always acts absolutely within the limits or the letter of the constitution, though to make this assumption is to substitute unreasonable hopes for rational expectations. What Englishmen should note, because they do not yet understand it, is that within the limits of the constitution the Irish Cabinet and the Irish Parliament possess and must possess the most extensive powers, and that these powers may be used in ways which would surprise and shock the British public, and impede and weaken the action of the Imperial, or English, Government.

D. The Restrictions (or Safeguards) and the Obligations

I. Their Nature.

The limitations on the power of the Irish Legislature are of a twofold character.

The Restrictions contained in clause 3 of the Bill are intended to restrain the Irish Parliament from acting as the representative body of an independent nation. This clause invalidates for example acts with respect to the Crown or the succession to the Crown, with respect to peace or war, with respect to the naval or military forces of the realm, with respect to treaties or other relations with foreign states, and with respect to trade with any place out of Ireland, which apparently includes the imposition of a protective tariff.

The Restrictions67 contained in clause 4 may be roughly divided into three heads; first, prohibitions intended to ensure the maintenance of absolute religious equality68; secondly, prohibitions intended to prevent injustice to individuals, such as deprivation of life, liberty, or property without due process of law, denial of equal protection of the law, the taxing of private property without due compensation, or the unfair treatment of any existing corporation; thirdly, a provision prohibiting any law which deprives any inhabitant of the United Kingdom of equal rights to public sea fisheries.69

On these Restrictions it were easy to write an elaborate treatise. Should our new constitution ever come into force, they will give rise to a whole series of judgments, and to lengthy books explanatory thereof. The language in which the Restrictions are expressed is in many cases exceptionable. No lawyer will venture to predict what for instance may be the interpretation placed by the Courts on such expressions as 'due process of law,' 'just compensation,' and the like, and it is more than doubtful whether the so-called safeguards are so expressed as to carry out the intention of their authors, or, even in words, adequately to protect either the authority of the Imperial Parliament or the rights of individuals. But it is not my purpose to criticise the Restrictions, or the Bill itself, in detail. The drafting of the Government of Ireland Bill needs much amendment, but at the present juncture it is waste of time to criticise defects removable by better draftmanship or by slight changes in the substance of the measure. My object is to dwell on such points relating to the Restrictions as show their bearing on the character of the new constitution.<u>70</u>

First. The Restrictions are one and all of them limits upon the powers of the Irish Parliament; they are none of them limits upon the powers of the Irish Executive. The new constitution does not contain—from its nature it hardly could contain—a single safeguard against abuse of power by the Irish Ministry or its servants. Yet in all countries there is far more reason to dread executive than parliamentary oppression, and this is emphatically true of Ireland.

Secondly. The Restrictions contain no prohibition against the passing of an Act of Indemnity.

Yet of all the laws which a Legislature can pass an Act of Indemnity is the most likely to produce injustice. It is on the face of it the legislation of illegality; the hope of it encourages acts of vigour, but it also encourages violations of law and of humanity. The tale of Flogging Fitzgerald in Ireland, or the history of Governor Eyre in Jamaica, is sufficient to remind us of the deeds of lawlessness and cruelty which in a period of civil conflict may be inspired by recklessness or panic, and may be pardoned by the retrospective sympathy or partisanship of a terror-stricken or vindictive Legislature. Circumstances no doubt may arise in Ireland, as in other countries, under which the maintenance of order or the protection of life may excuse or require deviation from the strict rules of legality. But the question, whether these circumstances have arisen, will always be decided far more justly by the Parliament at Westminster than it can be decided by the Parliament at Dublin. Can any one really maintain that a Parliament in which Mr. Healy, or, for that matter, Col. Saunderson, might be leader, would be as fair a tribunal as a Parliament under the guidance of Mr. Gladstone or Lord Salisbury for determining whether an officer who, acting under the direction of the Irish Government and with a view to maintain order at Belfast or at Dublin, should have put an agitator or conspirator to death without due trial, had or had not done his duty.

Thirdly. There is among the Restrictions no prohibition against the passing of an *ex post facto* law. Yet an *ex post facto* law is the instrument which a legislature is most apt to use for punishing the unpopular use of legal rights. There is not a landlord, there is not a magistrate, there is not a constable in Ireland, who may not tremble in fear of *ex post facto* legislation. There is no reason, as far as the Home Rule Bill goes, why the gaoler who kept Mr. William O'Brien in prison or the warders who attempted to pull off his breeches, should not be rendered legally liable to punishment for their offences against the unwritten law of Irish sedition. No such monstrosity of

47

legal inequity will, it may be said, be produced. I admit this. But the very object of prohibitions is the prevention of outrageous injustice. The wise founders of the United States prohibited both to Congress and to every State legislature the passing of *ex post facto* legislation. If any man hint that it be an insult to Ireland to anticipate the possible injustice of an Irish Parliament, my reply is simple. No Irishman need resent as an insult prohibitions which were not felt to be insulting either by the citizens of America or the citizens of Massachusetts.

Fourthly. The Restrictions on the powers of the Irish Parliament do not contain any safeguard against legislation which sets aside contracts.

This is remarkable, not to say ominous. The Gladstonian constitution has been drawn up by legislators who profess to profit by the experience of America. Under the Constitution of the United States71 no State can pass any law 'impairing the obligation of a contract.' This provision has kept alive throughout the Union the belief in the sacredness of legal promises. It embodies a principle which lies at the bottom of all progressive legislation. It gives the best guarantee which a constitution can give against the most insidious form of legislative unfairness; it embodies a doctrine which all legislatures are likely to neglect and which an Irish Parliament is more likely to neglect than any other legislature, for in Ireland there exist contracts which do not command popular approval, and the Imperial legislation of twenty years and more has taught the Irish people that agreements which do not command popular approval may, without breach of good faith, be set aside by legislative enactment. We all know further that reforms, or innovations, are desired by thousands of Irishmen which cannot be carried into effect unless the obligation of contracts be impaired. Why, then, have statesmen who borrow freely from the Constitution of the United States omitted the most salutary of its provisions from our new constitution?

The official reply is at any rate singular; it is apparently72 that the section of the United States Constitution which invalidates any law impairing the obligation of a contract has given much occupation to the Courts of America. This answer is on the face of it futile; it urges the proved utility of a law as a reason for its not being enacted; as well suggest that because the criminal courts are mainly occupied with the trial of thieves there ought to be no law against petty larceny, or that because the labours of the Divorce Court increase year by year, the law ought not to permit divorce. The absurdity of the official reply suggests the existence of some reason which the defenders of this strange omission are unwilling clearly to allege. The true reason why the founders of the new constitution have omitted in this instance to copy a polity which they profess to admire is not hard to discover. An enactment which enjoined an Irish Parliament to respect the sanctity of a contract would be fatal to any remodelling of the Irish land law which tended towards the spoliation of landowners. Yet this very fact makes the matter all the more serious. That British statesmen should under these circumstances deliberately decline to insert an injunction to respect the sanctity of plighted good faith is much more than an omission. It amounts to the suggestion, almost to the approval, of legislative robbery; it is a proclamation that as against landlords, as against creditors, as against any unpopular class, the Imperial Parliament sanctions the violation of good faith. To the Irish Parliament the authors of the new constitution in effect say: 'You may raise no soldiers, you may not yourselves summon volunteers for the defence of your country, you shall not impose customs on foreign goods, and are therefore forbidden to follow a policy of protection approved of by every civilised State except England; you shall neither establish nor endow a church, you shall not by providing salaries for your priesthood at once lighten the burdens of the flock, and improve the position of the pastor; these things, not to speak of many others, you are forbidden to do, though there are many wise statesmen who deem that the courses of action from which you are debarred would conduce to the dignity and the prosperity of Ireland; but there is one thing which you may do, you may sanction breach of faith, you may encourage dishonesty, you may enjoin fraud, you may continue to teach the worst lesson which the vacillation of English government has as yet taught the Irish people, you may drive home the conviction that no man need keep a covenant when the keeping thereof is to his own damage.' This is the message of political morality which the last true Parliament of the United Kingdom hands over to the first new Parliament of Ireland.

II. Their Enforcement.

The nature of the Restrictions imposed upon the Parliament, and indirectly upon the Government of Ireland, is of far less importance than are the means provided for their enforcement. A law which is not enforceable is a nullity; it has in strictness no existence.

The methods provided by the Home Rule Bill for keeping the Irish Parliament within its proper sphere of legislative activity are two in number—the veto of the Lord Lieutenant, and the action of the Courts.

The Veto. This is little more than an empty sham, for it must in general be exercised on the advice of the Irish Cabinet; in other words it will never be exercised at all.73 Were the matter not so serious there would be something highly amusing in the conduct of constitution-makers who, intending to provide against unconstitutional legislation on the part of the Irish Parliament, provide that the Irish Cabinet, who are practically appointed by the Irish Parliament, and who direct its legislation, shall have power to veto Bills passed by the Irish Parliament presumably on the advice of the Irish Cabinet.

The English Ministry no doubt may, if they see fit, instruct the Lord Lieutenant to veto a given Bill. So also the Imperial Parliament has authority to repeal or override any Act, constitutional or unconstitutional, passed by the Irish Parliament. Each power stands on the same footing, neither is meant for ordinary use; either is a means of legal revolution. The veto of the Crown means little in New Zealand; it will at best mean no more in Ireland; but in truth it will mean a good deal less. New Zealand sends no member to Westminster to stay the hand of the Imperial Government whenever it attempts by way of veto or otherwise to put in force the reserved powers of the Imperial Parliament.[74]

The Privy Council and the Courts. The English Privy Council[75] may nullify the effect of Irish legislation in two ways.

It may as an administrative body give a decision that an Act is void.[76] This power can by exercised only upon the application of the Lord Lieutenant or a Secretary of State, and it is a power which we may expect will be but rarely employed, for its use would at once give rise to a direct conflict between the Irish Parliament and the English Privy Council. Let it be noted in passing that this provision for the decision of constitutional questions is foreign to the habits and traditions of English Courts; no judge throughout the United Kingdom ever pronounces a speculative opinion upon the extent, operation, or validity of an Act of Parliament. It is the inveterate habit of our judges to deal with particular cases as they come before them, and with particular cases alone. They will find themselves greatly perplexed when they come to pronounce judgment upon abstract questions of law. This is not all. The proposed arrangement is as foreign to the spirit of American Federalism as it is to the spirit of English law. The Supreme Court of the United States never in strictness pronounces an Act either of Congress or of a State Legislature void. What the Court does is to treat it as void in the decision of a particular case. Tocqueville and other critics have directed special attention to the care with which the Federal tribunals, by dealing only with given cases as they arise, avoid as far as possible coming into conflict with any State. They determine the rights of individuals; they do not determine directly what may be the legislative competence of the State, or for that matter of the Federal, Legislature.[77] The extraordinary power given to the Privy Council violates a fundamental principle of federalism, which by the way is violated in other parts of the Home Rule Bill. It brings, or tends to bring, the central power, represented in this case by the Privy Council, into direct conflict with one of the States of the Federation.78

The English Privy Council, or, in strictness, the Judicial Committee of the Privy Council, is under the new constitution constituted a Final Court of Appeal from every Court in Ireland.79

The Privy Council also is the Court of Appeal from a new kind of Imperial, or as one may say 'Federal,' judiciary, specially formed for the determination of matters having relation to the competence of the Irish Parliament.

This Imperial or Federal judiciary consists of the two Exchequer Judges of the Supreme Court in Ireland; they are appointed under the Great Seal of the United Kingdom, and therefore by the English Ministry. Their salaries are charged on the Consolidated Fund of the United Kingdom, and they are removable only on an address to the Houses of the Imperial Parliament. They constitute therefore an Imperial not an Irish Court. Before this Court may be brought on the application of any party thereto any legal proceedings in Ireland which *inter alia* 'touch any matter not within the power of the Irish Legislature, or touch any matter affected by a law which the Irish Legislature has not power to repeal or alter.'80 With the details of these arrangements I need not trouble my readers; the point to notice is that, whenever in any proceeding in Ireland the validity or constitutionality of an Irish Act can come into question, the matter may, at the wish of any party concerned, and in many cases apparently must be, brought before an Imperial or in effect British Court —the Exchequer Judges—and be determined by them subject to an appeal to another Imperial or British Court, viz. the Privy Council. Note further that to the Exchequer Judges are given special powers for the enforcement of any judgment of their Court. If the Sheriff does not give effect to their judgment, they may appoint any other officer with the full rights of a Sheriff to enforce it.81

Here then we have the machinery of the Imperial, or Federal, Judicature. To put the matter simply, the Restrictions imposed on the Irish Parliament depend for their effectiveness on judgments of the Privy Council enforced by the Exchequer Judges.

Consider how the whole arrangement will work.82 The theoretical operation of the scheme is clear enough. *A* sues *X* in an Irish Court, say, to simplify matters, before the Exchequer Judges, for £1,000 due to *A* for rent. *X* bases his defence on an Act of the Irish Parliament, drawn by Irish statesmen, and approved presumably by Irish electors. *A* questions the constitutionality of the Act. The Exchequer Judges are divided in opinion. The matter at last comes before the Privy Council. The Privy Council pronounce the Act void, and give judgment in *A's* favour. He has a right to recover the £1,000 from *X*. The whole question in theory is settled. The law is unconstitutional, the law is void; *A* has obtained judgment. But can the judgment be enforced? This is the essential question; for the object of a plaintiff is to obtain not judgment but payment or execution. What then are the means for enforcing the judgment of the Privy Council when it is not supported by Irish opinion, when it sets aside an Act of the Irish Parliament, and when it may possibly be opposed to the decision, in a similar case, of an Irish Court? The means are the action of the Sheriff. What if the Sheriff is a strong Nationalist, and makes default? The only thing to be done is to appoint an officer empowered to carry out the decree of the Court. Of course if the Irish Ministry are bent on enforcing the judgment, if the Exchequer Court, whose judgment, it may be, has been overruled, is zealous in supporting the authority of the Privy Council, if the Irish people are filled with reverence for tribunals which are really English Courts, all will go well. But Mr. Gladstone himself cannot anticipate that novel constitutional machinery will work with ease, or that on the passing of the Home Rule Bill the disposition, the traditional feelings, and the sympathies of the Irish populace will be changed. Suppose that *A* is Lord Clanricarde; suppose that *X* is an evicted tenant. It is not common sense to believe that the judgment in his lordship's favour will as a matter of course take effect. At the present moment the Irish Courts, backed by the whole authority of the Imperial Government and the Irish Executive, often find a difficulty in enforcing their judgments. Will English Courts find it easy to give effect to a judgment in Ireland if the Irish Executive and its servants stand neutral or hostile? What if the Irish House of Commons turn out as unwilling that force should be used for enforcing the decree of the Privy Council as are some English Radicals that force shall be employed for the protection of free labourers against Trades Unionists? What if the officer of the Court is in fact some bailiff trembling for his own life? He may, I am told, call in the military. Of his authority to do this I am not quite sure. He must, I suppose, in the first instance apply to the Irish Home Secretary. The Irish Minister pressed by the opposition turns a deaf ear to the appeal of the bailiff. Application must then be made in some form or other to the English Ministry. The Imperial Cabinet will think more than once before horse, foot, and artillery are, against the wish of the Irish Government, put in movement to enforce the judgment of a British Court, and to obtain £1,000 for Lord Clanricarde. The matter will have become serious; the dignity of the Irish nation will be at stake; the complaints of the plaintiff will be drowned by the indignant clamours of eighty members at Westminster. The essential principle of the new constitution is that there shall be but one Executive in Ireland. The moment that the British Government intervenes to support the judgment of British Courts, we have in Ireland two hostile Executives. We tremble on the verge either of legal revolution or of civil war. An English Cabinet, I suspect, will hardly enforce the unpopular rights of a hated plaintiff by use of arms.

Why, it will be said, assume that the Irish Government and the Irish people will not enforce the law? The assumption, I answer, is justified not only by the history of Ireland, but by general experience. In all federations, even the best ordered, difficulties constantly arise as to the sphere of the Federal Government and the State Governments, and as to the enforcement of judgments delivered by Federal Courts. The authority of the federal tribunals has not always been easily enforced even in the United States. Serious difficulties hamper the action of the Swiss federal authorities. Even in England enthusiasm or conviction occasionally triumphs over legality. English clergymen are at least as reasonable as excited politicians, yet Ritualists have not invariably submitted to the authority of the Privy Council. Why should Irishmen be more reasonable than other men? In Ireland we are trying an entirely novel and dangerous experiment; we are fostering the spirit of nationality under the forms of federation. The Privy Council, hide the matter as you will, represents British power. If Ireland is a nation, the Government of Great Britain is an alien Government; the judgments of the Privy Council are the judgments of an alien Court, and reason forbids us to expect more submission to the decisions of an alien tribunal than to the laws of an alien legislature.

Suppose, however, that British judgments are enforced by the British army. Is this a result in which any Englishman or Irishman could rejoice? Can we say that the new constitution works well when its real and visible sanction is the use of British soldiers? The plain truth is that arrangements for legally restraining the Irish Parliament within the due limits of its powers must be ineffective and unreal and, if the principle of Home Rule be once admitted, the widest must be the wisest form of it. Colonial independence is better for Ireland and safer for England than sham federalism.83

Grant, however, that the judgments of the Privy Council can be enforced more easily than I suppose, still even Gladstonians would admit that the proper working of the new constitution depends on two presumptions. The one is that the Irish people are under no strong temptation to oppose the Restrictions or to throw off the obligations imposed upon the Irish Parliament or Government. The other that they possess no ready means for nullifying these Restrictions or obligations.

Each of these assumptions is false.

Restraints ineffective for the protection either of British interests or of individual freedom may be intensely irritating to national sentiment.

The limitations imposed on the powers of the Irish Parliament, or, in other words, of the Irish people, are opposed to the spirit of nationality and independence which Home Rule, it is hoped, will appease or satisfy. They will be hateful therefore not only to that multitude whom Gladstonians call the Irish people, but to every Irishman who is bidden by Gladstonians to consider himself a member of the Irish nation.

The Irish are a martial race; they excel in the practice, and delight in the pageantry, of warfare, but they are forbidden to raise a regiment or man a gunboat. They cannot legally raise a regiment of volunteers, they cannot save their country from invasion. Will they permanently acquiesce in restraints not imposed on the Channel Islands? Irishmen, Unionists no less than Home Rulers, are mostly Protectionists, and believe that tariffs may give to Ireland, not indeed a 'plethora of wealth,' for of this no man out of Bedlam except Mr. Gladstone dreams, but reasonable prosperity. Vain to argue that Protection is folly. Englishmen think so, and Englishmen are right. But English doctrine is not accepted in Germany, in France, in the United States, or in the British Colonies; why should Irishmen be wiser than the inhabitants of every civilised country, except England? The fact, in any case, cannot be altered that most Home Rulers are Protectionists, and that many of them desire Home Rule mainly because they desire Protection for Ireland. Yet Protection, at any rate in the form of a tariff, they cannot have.84 Take again the Restrictions imposed on the endowment of religion. All English Nonconformists, and many English Churchmen, hold these Restrictions to be in themselves politic and just. But the one strong reason for the concession of Home Rule is that Irishmen disagree with English notions of policy and of justice. No one can assign any reason why Irish statesmen, Catholics or Protestants, might not feel it a matter of duty or of policy to endow the priesthood, to level up instead of levelling down, to enter into some sort of concordat with Rome. It is a policy which is distasteful to English Nonconformists and to most Irish Protestants. But under a system of Home Rule, at any rate, English Nonconformists have no right to dictate the policy of Ireland. There is not the remotest reason why Restrictions on the endowments of religion and the like should not be hateful to Irishmen.

The limitations, in short, on the competence of the Irish Parliament are inconsistent with the fundamental principle of Gladstonian statecraft. It is a policy we are told of trust in the people, the limitations are dictated by distrust of the Irish people; Home Rule is to be granted in order that Irishmen may give effect to Irish ideas; the Restrictions are enacted to check the development of Irish ideas, and to impose English ideas upon the policy of Ireland.

As though, however, the Restraints were not enough to cause first irritation and then agitation, the financial provisions contemplated by the Bill are in themselves certain to generate, not future, but immediate discord.

Of the financial arrangements instituted under the new constitution, my purpose is to say very little. My object is not to show that Mr. Gladstone's financial calculations are wrong, or that they are ruinous to Ireland or unfair to England. All this is for my present purpose immaterial. My aim is to insist that, in their very nature, they are a cause of conflict; and that they bring the interest, and, even more, the sentiment, of Ireland into direct opposition with the power of England.85

All the customs payable at every Irish port are to be regulated, collected, and managed by, and to be paid into, the Exchequer of the United Kingdom. Not a penny of these customs benefits Ireland; they are all—and this is certainly the light in which they will appear to most Irishmen—a contribution to the revenue of the United Kingdom, that is, of England. If every taxable article were smuggled into Ireland, so that not one pound of Irish customs were paid to the English treasury, the Imperial power would lose, but the Irish State would gain. Ireland would be delivered from a tax which will soon be called a tribute. If, moreover, Ireland continues to be treated as financially a part of the United Kingdom, then free smuggling, which is free trade, would make Ireland a free port, where might be landed untaxed the goods required by the whole United Kingdom. It is easy to see how the English revenue would suffer, but it is equally easy to see that Irish commerce might flourish. If I am told that the ruin of the British revenue may be averted by the examination of goods brought from Ireland to Great Britain—this, of course, is so. But then freedom of trade within the United Kingdom is at an end. We are compelled, in substance, to raise an internal line of custom houses; we abolish at one stroke one great benefit of the Treaty of Union.

The mode, again, in which the customs are levied outrages every kind of national sentiment. Coast-guards, custom-house officers, and gaugers are never popular among a population of smugglers; they will not be the more beloved when every custom-house officer or coastguard is the representative of an alien power, and is employed to levy tribute from Ireland.

Another leading feature of the financial arrangements is the charging upon the Irish Consolidated Fund of various sums rightly due and payable to the Exchequer of the United Kingdom.86 They are made a first charge upon the revenue of Ireland. They are to be paid in the last resort upon the order of the Lord Lieutenant, acting as an Imperial officer. The necessity for some arrangement of this kind is clear. Millions have been lent to Ireland, and these millions must be repaid. But if the need for some such arrangement be certain, its desperate impolicy is no less certain. England and Ireland, the English Government and the Irish Government, are brought into direct hostile collision. The rich English Government appears in the light of an imperious creditor the Irish Government stands in the position of a poverty-stricken debtor. Note, and this is the point which should be pressed home, that in all confederations the difficulty of exacting the money needed by the federal government from any state of the confederacy has been found all but insuperable. Study the history of the thirteen American colonies between the time of the acknowledgment of their independence by England and the formation of the United States. This has been termed 'the critical period' of American history. The colonies were united by recollections of common suffering and of common triumph, they were not divided by race or religion; no State aspired to separate nationality, yet they drifted rapidly towards anarchy; they were discontented at home, they were powerless abroad, above all, they nearly made shipwreck on the financial arrangements. Congress was never able, for the satisfaction either of national needs or of national honour, to obtain fair contributions from the different States.[87]

Already, further, before the Home Rule Bill has passed from the hands of the House of Commons Mr. Gladstone's very moderate demands, as they seem to Englishmen, are held by some Irish Nationalists to be outrageous.[88] The difference, moreover, is not a matter of calculation, to be settled by accounts and balances, or disposed of by auditors. No one can read the statements of Nationalists such as Mr. Redmond or Mr. Clancy without seeing that the real difference of view lies very deep. These typical Nationalists do not regard the United Kingdom as a nation. Ireland is the nation. They doubt what is her interest in the British Empire; they believe, and already hint, that the financial arrangements between the two countries cannot be treated as a mere pecuniary transaction. Ireland has been overtaxed and overburdened. She has claims for compensation. All the feelings or convictions which inspired hatred of Irish landlords are already being aroused with regard to the Imperial power. A campaign against tribute may become as popular as a campaign against rent. The two campaigns indeed have a close affinity; a large portion of the tribute is in reality payment in respect of rent, and the instalments which an Irish farmer pays to buy his land will, to him at any rate, appear rent or tribute payable to Great Britain. The rent or tribute will be collected under the new constitution by the Irish Government.[89] No Irish Ministry will relish the position of collector. It would have been difficult for a landlord to collect rent after his agent had publicly announced that it was excessive and unjust. Yet a landlord could dismiss his agent; the English Cabinet cannot dismiss the Irish Government. It is certain too that the Irish Ministry will not find the collection of rent easy. Should the Irish Government state that the rent is iniquitously high, and refuse to collect it, what will be the position of the British Ministry? It must either set the constitution aside or undertake for itself the collection of rent in opposition to, or, at any rate, unaided by, the

Irish Executive and the Irish Parliament. No more odious task was ever undertaken by a government. Suppose, however, that things do not come to the worst, the financial arrangements of the Bill ensure that Ireland will soon demand modifications of its provisions. Opposition is a probability, discontent is a certainty.

Ireland is provided under the new constitution with the readiest means of nullifying the Restrictions. The Irish Cabinet and its servants can at any moment reduce an unpopular law to a nullity. Even in England a resolution of the House of Commons may be enough to turn a law into a dead letter. The Imperial Cabinet at this moment could go very near making the Vaccination Acts of no effect, and by declining to have troops sent to Hull could, as I have already pointed out, give victory to the Trades Unionists. Nor is it necessary that the Cabinet should decline sending forces to Hull for the support of the law. An intimation that persons accused of intimidation would either not be prosecuted at all, or if prosecuted and convicted, would be pardoned, would be sufficient of itself to make the strike successful. In no country could the Executive do more to render laws ineffectual than in Ireland. The Irish Cabinet might by mere inaction render the collection of rent impossible; they might, as I have already pointed out, give tacit encouragement to smuggling. If the people regarded a coastguard as an enemy, if he and his family were left severely alone, if he were often maltreated and occasionally shot, his position might be a difficult one, even if supported by the whole force of the state. But if smuggling were regarded as no crime, if the smuggler were looked upon as the patriot who deprived an alien power of a revenue to which England had no right, it is clear that nothing but the energetic support of all the central and local authorities in the country could give a revenue officer the remotest chance of victory in his contest with smugglers. But suppose the national government were apathetic, suppose that the Irish Ministry looked with favourable eye on the diminution of English revenue; suppose that no Irish official gave any aid to a custom-house officer; suppose that, if a British coastguardsman were murdered, Irish detectives made no effort to discover the wrong-doer; and that when the culprit was discovered the Irish law officers hesitated to prosecute; suppose that when a prosecution took place the Attorney-General showed that his heart was not in the matter, and that the jury acquitted a ruffian clearly guilty of murder, is it not as clear as day that smuggling would flourish and no customs be collected? In the same way the Irish Ministry might by mere apathy, by the very easy process of doing nothing, nullify the effect of judgments delivered by the Exchequer judges, and the Irish Ministry would show very little ingenuity if they could not without any open breach of the law impede the carrying out of executions against the goods of persons whom popular feeling treated as patriots.

The Irish Executive might, as already pointed out,90 easily raise an Irish army. Drilling countenanced or winked at by the Irish Ministry could never be stopped by the British Government. Prussia at the period of her extreme weakness, and under the jealous eye of Napoleon, sent every Prussian through the ranks. Bulgaria raised an army while pretending to encourage athletic sports. The value of the precedent is not likely to escape an Irish Premier.

The Irish Parliament cannot legally repeal a single provision of the constitution, but an Irish Parliament might render much of the constitution a nullity. The Parliament might pass Acts which trenched upon the Restrictions limiting its authority. Till treated as void such statutes would be the law of the land. Such voidable Acts, and even parliamentary resolutions,91 would go like a watchword through the country and encourage throughout Ireland popular resistance to Imperial law. A profound observer has remarked that people do not reckon highly enough the importance at a revolutionary crisis of any show or appearance of legality.92 Revolution acquires new force when masked under the form of law. This is a point which Englishmen constantly overlook. They know the moral influence of leagues and combinations; they do not reflect that a Parliament or House of Commons in sympathy with resistance to Imperial demands would possess tenfold the moral authority of any National League. Note too that the Irish Ministry and the Irish Parliament would play into one another's hands, and would further be strengthened by their Irish allies at Westminster, as also by the Irish electoral vote in England.

For the true stronghold of the Irish Government lies, under the new constitution, at Westminster.93

There they would command at least eighty votes: the Irish members could still, as now, and far more effectively than now, coerce under ordinary circumstances any Ministry disposed to enforce the rights of the Imperial Government, or, in other words, of England.

Take a concrete case to which I have already referred.94 Irish farmers who have purchased under the Ashbourne Act grow weary of paying instalments which are equivalent to rent. The Irish Cabinet refuses to collect the rent; it urges its absolute inability to pay the sums due to the Imperial Exchequer and asks for remission. Meanwhile the Irish House of Commons passes a resolution supporting the conduct of the Irish Government. The British Ministers are stern, and reject the request of the Irish Cabinet. The Cabinet at Dublin retire from office. No successors can be appointed who command the support of the Irish Parliament. The Lord Lieutenant advises the Government at home that things have come to a deadlock and that a dissolution will change nothing. Thereupon the Irish members at Westminster begin to move; they threaten general hostility to the British Ministry.

They proffer their support to the Opposition. It may of course happen that the British Ministry can, like the Unionist Government of 1886, defy the Opposition and the Irish members combined. If so the English Cabinet can risk a constitutional conflict in Ireland, though it is a conflict likely to end in disturbance or civil war. But judging the future by the past the eighty members will hold the balance of power. If so their course is clear. They expel from office the Ministers who have protected the rights of the Imperial Government. A weak Ministry depending on Irish votes rules, or rather is ruled, at Downing Street. Every one knows how, under the supposed conditions, the affair will end. There will be a transaction of some sort, and we may be certain that such a transaction will be to the advantage of the Irish Government, and will weaken or discredit Imperial or English authority. We come round here to the root of the whole matter. Were the Restrictions on the power of the Irish Parliament real and easily enforceable, were the obligations imposed upon or undertaken by the Irish people obligations of which an English Ministry could at once compel the fulfilment, Restrictions and obligations alike would be rendered futile and unreal by the presence of the Irish members at Westminster. Every Home Rule scheme which can be proposed is impolitic and is as dangerous as Separation; but the most impolitic of all possible forms of Home Rule is the scheme embodied in the Bill of 1893. Its special and irremediable flaw is the retention of the Irish members at Westminster. This governs and vitiates all the leading provisions of the new constitution. Under its influence every conceivable safeguard, the supreme authority of Parliament, the veto, the legal restrictions on the competence of the Irish legislature melt away into nothing.

They are some of them capable of doing harm, they are none of them capable of doing good.

Cast a glance back at the leading features of the new constitution.

The Imperial Parliament remains in form unchanged, and retains the attribute of nominal sovereignty. But in Ireland the Imperial Parliament surrenders all, or nearly all, the characteristics of true and effective power; it retains in fact in Ireland nothing more than the right to effect under the semblance of a legal proceeding a revolution which after all must be carried out by force. For practical purposes it has no more power at Dublin than it has at Melbourne, *i.e.* it retains at Dublin scarcely any real power whatever.

For the sake of this nominal and shadowy authority the Imperial Parliament is itself transformed into a strange cross between a British Parliament and the Congress of an Anglo-Irish Federation.

The Irish Executive and the Irish Parliament become under the new constitution the true and real Government of Ireland. But the Irish

Government and the Irish people are fettered by Restrictions which would not be borne by the Government or the people of a self-governing colony. These Restrictions are ineffective to bind, but they are certain to gall, and if taken together with onerous financial obligations to Great Britain, which whether just or not must have an air of hardness, and with the habitual presence in Ireland of a British army under the direction of the British Executive, lay an ample foundation for the most irritating of conflicts.

The new constitution, lastly, places in the hands of the Irish people ample means for constitutional or extra-constitutional resistance to Imperial, or in fact to English, power, and almost ensures the success of Ireland in any constitutional conflict. The presence of the Irish members at Westminster saves, or proclaims, the nominal sovereignty of the Imperial Parliament; but their presence in truth makes this sovereignty unexercisable, and therefore worthless, and while increasing the apparent power ensures the real weakness of England.

Chapter III—Why The New Constitution Will Not Be A Settlement Of The Irish Question

*'We believe that this measure [the Home Rule Bill] when improved in Committee will be, at all events in our time, a final settlement of the Irish question.'*95

'Five speeches were made from the Irish benches ... there was not one of those speeches which fell short of what we have declared to be in our opinion necessary for the acceptance of this Bill. That is where we look for a durable and solid statement as to finality. We find the word *finality* not even eschewed by the generous unreserve of the honourable member for North Longford96 who attached the character of finality to the Bill.... What said the honourable member for Kerry97 last night? He said, *"This is a Bill that will end the feud of ages"* This is exactly what we want to do. That is what I call acceptance by the Irish members of this Bill.... *What we mean by this Bill is to close and bury a controversy of seven hundred years.'*98

This hope of ending the feud of ages has been for years dangled by Gladstonians before the English electorate. It has gained thousands of votes for Home Rule. But it is doomed to disappointment. The new constitution will never be a settlement of the Irish question: and this for three reasons, which can be definitely stated and easily understood.

First. The new constitution satisfies neither Ireland nor England.

It does not satisfy Ireland.

Ulster, Protestant Ireland, and indeed, speaking generally, all men of property in Ireland, whether Protestant or Catholic, detest Home Rule. They hate the new constitution, they protest against the new constitution, they assert that they will to the utmost of their ability resist the introduction and impede the working of the new constitution. Their abhorrence of Home Rule may be groundless, their threats may be baseless; their power to give effect to their menaces may have no existence. All that I now contend is that the strongest, and the most energetic, part of Irish society is in fact and in truth bitterly opposed, not only to the details, but to the fundamental principle, of the new polity. It avails nothing to urge that the Protestants and the educated Catholics are in a minority. This plea shows that in Parliament they can be outvoted; it does not show that they will, or can, be pacified by a policy which runs counter to their traditions, their interests, and their sentiment. You cannot vote men into content, you cannot coerce them into satisfaction. Let us look facts in the face. The measure which is supposed to gratify Ireland satisfies at most a majority of Irishmen. This may be enough for a Parliamentary tactician, it is not enough for a far-seeing statesman or a man of plain common sense. When we are told a minority are filled with discontent, we must ask who constitute the minority. When we find that the minority consists of men of all descriptions and of all creeds, that they represent the education, the respectability, the worth, and the wealth of Ireland, we must be filled with alarm. Wealth, no doubt, is no certain sign of virtue, any more than poverty can be identified with vice; a rich man may be a scoundrel, and a poor man may be an honour to the human race, but the world would be much worse constituted than it is, if the possession of a competence were not connected with honesty, energy, adherence to duty, and every other civic virtue. When it is said or admitted by Gladstonians that the propertied classes of Ireland are against Home Rule we know what this means; it means that the energy of Ireland is against Home Rule, that the honesty of Ireland is against Home Rule, that the learning of Ireland is against Home Rule, that all that makes a nation great is against Home Rule, and that the Irishmen most entitled to our respect and honour implore us not to force upon them the curse of Home Rule. This is no trifle. Let us at any rate have done with phrases; let us admit that the satisfaction of Ireland means merely the satisfaction of a class, though it may be the most numerous class of Irishmen, and that it also means the bitter discontent of the one class of Irishmen who are specially loyal to Great Britain. If we are closing one feud we are assuredly opening another feud which it may at least be as hard to heal.

But is it true that even the Home Rulers of Ireland are satisfied? Their representatives indeed accept the new constitution. Their acceptance may well, as far as intention goes, be honest. Mr. Davitt, I dare say, when he sentimentalises in the House of Commons about his affection for the English democracy, is nearly, though not quite, as sincere as when he used to express passionate hatred of England.[99] But acquiescence is one thing, satisfaction is another. There is every reason why the Irish members should acquiesce in the new constitution. They obtain much, and they gain the means of getting more. Quite possibly they feel grateful. But their gratitude is not the gratitude of Ireland, and gratitude is hardly a sentiment possible, or indeed becoming, to a nation.

England saved Portugal and Spain from the domination of France. Do we find that Portuguese and Spaniards gladly subordinate their interests to the welfare of England? France delivered Italy from thraldom to Austria; French blood paid the price of Italian freedom. Yet France is detested from one end of Italy to the other, whilst Italians rejoice in the alliance with Austria. In all this there is nothing unreasonable and nothing to blame. Policy is not sentimentality, and the relations of peoples cannot be regulated in the same manner as the relations of individuals. Thirty, twenty, ten, five years hence all the sentiment of the year 1893 will have vanished. Irish content and satisfaction must, if it is to exist at all, rest on a far more solid basis than the hopes, the words, the pledges, or the intentions of Mr. M'Carthy, Mr. Sexton, or Mr. Davitt. Note that their satisfaction is even now of a limited kind. It absolutely depends on the new constitution being worked exactly in the way which they desire. The use of the veto, legislation for Ireland by the Imperial Parliament, any conflict between the wish of England and the wish, I do not say of Ireland, but of the Irish Nationalists, must from the nature of things put an end to all gratitude or content. But we may go further than this: the new constitution contains elements of discord. It denies to Ireland the rights of a nation; it does not concede to her the full privileges of colonial independence. No genuine Nationalist can really acquiesce in the prohibition of Ireland's arming even in self-defence. Where, again, is the Nationalist who is prepared to say that he will not if the Bill is passed demand that every conspirator and every dynamiter, who is suffering for the cause of Ireland, shall be released from prison? Is it credible that the Land Leaguers have forgotten what is due to the wounded soldiers of their cause? Are they prepared to forget the imperative claims of evicted tenants or imprisoned zealots?[100] I cannot believe it.

But if they are so base as to forget what is due to their friends and victims, what trust could England place in the permanence of any sentiment expressed by such men with however much temporary fervour and however much apparent honesty? If, as I am convinced, the Irish leaders are not prepared to betray the fanatics or ruffians who have trusted and served them, then with what content does England look on the prospect of a general amnesty for criminals or of lavish rewards for breach of contract and the defiance of law?

But in truth the new constitution provides for the general discontent, not of one class of Irishmen, but of the whole Irish people.

Home Rule is at bottom federalism, and the successful working of a federal government depends on the observation by its founders of two principles. The first is that no one State should be so much more powerful than the rest as to be capable of vying in strength with the whole, or even with many of them combined.[101] The second is that the federal power should never if possible come into direct conflict with the authority of any State. Each of these well-known principles has, partly from necessity and partly from want of skill, been violated by the constructors of the spurious federation which is to be miscalled the United Kingdom. The confederacy will consist of two States; the one, England, to use popular but highly significant language, in wealth, in population, and in prestige immensely outweighs the other, Ireland. And by an error less excusable because it might have been avoided, the power of the central government will be brought into direct conflict with the authority of the Irish State. Read the Bill as it should be read by any one who wishes to understand the working of the new constitution, and throughout substitute 'England' for the term 'United Kingdom.' Note then what must be the operation of the constitution in the eyes of an Irishman. The federal power is the power of England. An English Viceroy instructed by an English Ministry will veto Bills passed by an Irish Parliament and approved by the Irish people. An English court will annul Irish Acts; English revenue officers will collect Irish customs, and every penny of the Irish customs will pass into the English Exchequer. An English army commanded by English officers, acting under the orders of English ministers, will be quartered up and down Ireland, and, in the last resort, English soldiers will be employed to wring money from the Irish Exchequer for the rigorous payment of debts due from Ireland to England. Will any Irishman of spirit bear this? Will not Irishmen of all creeds and parties come to hate the constitution which subjects Ireland to English rule when England shall have in truth been turned into an alien power?

The new constitution does not in any case satisfy England.

That England is opposed to Home Rule is admitted on all hands; that England has good reason to oppose the new form of Home Rule with very special bitterness is apparent to every Unionist, and must soon become apparent to any candid man, whether Gladstonian or Unionist, who carefully studies the provisions of the new constitution, and meditates on the effect of retaining Irish representatives in the Parliament at Westminster. For my present purpose there is no need to establish that English discontent is reasonable; enough to note its existence.

A consideration must be here noticed which as the controversy over Home Rule goes on will come into more and more prominence. We are engaged in rearranging new terms of union between England and Ireland; this is the real effect of the Home Rule Bill; but for such a rearrangement Great Britain and Ireland must in fairness, no less than in logic, be treated as independent parties. Whether you make a Union or remodel a Union between two countries the satisfaction of both parties to the treaty is essential. Till England is satisfied the new constitution lacks moral sanction. That the Act of Union could not have been carried without, at any rate, the technical assent both of Great Britain and Ireland is admitted, and yet the moral validity of the Treaty of Union is, whether rightly or not, after the lapse of ninety-three years assailed, on the ground that the assent of Ireland was obtained by fraud and undue influence. But if the separate assent of both parties was required for the making of the treaty, so the free assent of both must be required for its revision, and the politicians who force on Great Britain the terms of a political partnership which Great Britain rejects, repeat in 1893 and in an aggravated form the error or crime of 1800.102

Secondly. The new constitution rests on an unsound foundation.

It is a topsy-turvy constitution, it aims at giving weakness supremacy over strength.

The main, though not the sole, object of a well-constituted polity is to place political power (whilst guarding against its abuse) in the hands of the men, or body of men, who from the nature of things, *i.e.* by wealth, education, position, numbers, or otherwise, form the most powerful portion of a given state. The varying forms of the English Constitution have, on the whole, possessed the immense merit of giving at each period of our history political authority into the hands of the class, or classes, who made up the true strength of the nation. Right has in a rough way been combined with might. Wherever this is not the case, and genuine power is not endowed with political authority, there exists a sure cause of revolution; for sooner or later the natural forces of any society must assert their predominance. No institution will stand which does not correspond with the nature of things. Vain were all the efforts of party interest or of philanthropic enthusiasm to give to the Blacks political predominance in the Southern States. Votes, ballot boxes, laws, federal arms, all were in vain. By methods which no man will justify, but which no power could resist, the Whites have re-acquired political authority. The nature of things could not be made obedient to the dogmas of democratic equality. Now the gravest flaw of the new constitution, the disease from which it is certain to perish, is that, in opposition to the forces which ultimately must determine the destiny of the United Kingdom, it renders the strong elements of the community subordinate to the weak.

In Ireland Dublin is made supreme over Belfast, the South is made not the equal, but in effect the master of the North; ignorance is given dominion over education, poverty is allowed to dispose of wealth. If Ireland were an independent state, or even a self-governed British colony, things would right themselves. But the politicians who are to rule in Dublin will not depend upon their own resources or be checked by a sense of their own feebleness. They will be constitutionally and legally entitled to the support of the British army; they will constitute the worst form of government of which the world has had experience, a government which relying for its existence on the aid of an external power finds in its very feebleness support for tyranny. Murmurs are already heard of armed resistance. These mutterings, we are told, are nothing but bluster. It is at any rate that sort of "bluster" at which the justice and humanity of a loyal Englishman must take alarm. I have not yet learnt to look without horror on the possibility of civil war, nor to picture to myself without emotion the situation of brave men compelled by the British army to obey rulers whose moral claim to allegiance they justly deny and whose power unaided by British arms they contemn. Civil warfare created by English policy and despotism maintained by English arms must surely be to any Englishman objects of equal abhorrence.

But in England no less than in Ireland our new constitution gives artificial power to weakness. At Westminster the Irish members, be they 80 or 103, will have no legitimate place. Mr. Gladstone on this point is, for aught I know, at one with the Unionists. In 1886 he without scruple, and therefore no doubt without any sense of injustice, expelled the representatives of Ireland from the British Parliament. In 1893 he brings them back to Westminster. But his words betray his hesitation. He expects, may we not say he hopes, that they will remain in Ireland and on their occasional visits to London have the good sense and good taste not to interfere in British affairs. Few are the persons who share these anticipations. If they are to be realised they must be embodied in the constitution; the Premier might at this moment without shame, and without regret, revert to the better policy of 1886. On his present policy we all know that his expectations will not be fulfilled. The voluntary absence of the Irish members from Westminster is as vain a dream as the fancy that Ireland under Home Rule may suffer from a plethora of money. To Westminster the Irish members will come. If they do not come of their own accord they will be fetched by allies who need their help. At Westminster they will hold the balance of parties, and will while the constitution lasts rule the destiny of England with a sole regard at best to the immediate interest of Ireland, at worst to the interests of an Irish faction. To Ireland will be given power without responsibility, to England will belong responsibility without power. Nor will the unnatural subjection of a great, a flourishing, a wealthy, and a proud country to a weaker and poorer neighbour be rendered the more bearable by the knowledge that the ill-starred supremacy of Ireland means, in England, the equally unnatural and equally ominous predominance of an English faction, which, since it needs Irish aid, does not command England's confidence. Radicals or revolutionists will in the long run have bitter cause to regret an arrangement which identifies their political triumph with England's humiliation.

Thirdly. The new constitution is based on a play of words which conceals two contradictory interpretations of its character.103

The supremacy of the Imperial Parliament means to Irish Home Rulers and to most Gladstonians that Ireland shall possess colonial independence.104 It means to Unionists and to many electors who can hardly be called either

Unionists or Gladstonians, that the British Parliament, or, in other words, England, shall retain the real, effective, and even habitual control of Irish affairs. In the one sense it means only that Ireland shall remain part of the British Empire, in the other that Ireland shall still be part of the United Kingdom. And, what is of great importance, the mass of Englishmen waver between these two interpretations of Imperial supremacy. When they think of Home Rule as satisfying Ireland, they hold that it gives Irishmen everything which they can possibly ask. When they think of Home Rule as not dismembering the United Kingdom, they fancy that it leaves to the British Parliament all the real authority which Parliament can possibly require.

This difference of interpretation lays the foundation of misunderstanding, but it does far more harm than this. It must keep Irish Nationalists alarmed, and not without reason, for the permanence of the independence which they may have obtained. A change of feeling or a change of party may cause the Imperial Parliament to assert its reserved authority. England keeps her pledges.105 Yes, but here it is not a mere question of good faith. When two contractors each from the beginning put *bona fide* a different interpretation upon their contract, neither of them is chargeable with dishonesty for acting in accordance with his own view of the agreement. The spirit of Unionism and the spirit of Separation will survive the creation of the new constitution. Under one form or another Unionists will be opposed to Federalists and it is more than possible, should the Bill pass, that the division of English parties may turn upon their reading of the Irish Government Act, 1893.

The possibility, again, that the Parliament at Westminster may assert its reserved authority, if it raises the fears of Irishman, may excite the hopes of English politicians. If at any time the supremacy of Ireland becomes unbearable to British national sentiment, or if the condition of Ireland menaces or is thought to menace English interests, the new constitution places in the hands of a British majority a ready-made weapon for the restoration of British power. The result might be attained without the necessity for passing any Act of Parliament, or of repealing a single section of the Irish Government Act, 1893. A strong Viceroy might be sent to Ireland; he might be instructed not to convoke the Irish Parliament at all; or, having convoked, at once to prorogue it. He might thereupon form any Ministry he chose out of the members of the Irish Privy Council. The Imperial Parliament would at once resume its present position and could pass laws for Ireland. This might be called revolution or reaction. For my argument it matters not two straws by what name this policy be designated. The scheme sketched out is not a policy which I recommend. My contention is not that it will be expedient—this is a matter depending upon circumstances which no man can foresee—but that it will be strictly and absolutely legal.

The supremacy of the Imperial Parliament, combined with the presence of the Irish members at Westminster, will thus by a curious fatality turn out a source at once of permanent disquietude to Ireland and of immediate, if not of permanent, weakness to England.

Our New Constitution is not made to last Home Rule does not close a controversy; it opens a revolution.

No one in truth expects that the new constitution will stand. Its very builders hesitate when they speak of its permanence,106 and are grateful for the generous credulity of a friend who believes in its finality. Nor is it hard to conjecture (and in such a matter nothing but conjecture is possible) what are the forces or tendencies which threaten its destruction.

If Ireland is discontented Irishmen will demand either the extension of federalism or separation. In every federal government the tendency of the States is to diminish as far as possible the authority of the federal power. But this tendency will be specially strong in the grotesque Anglo-Irish federation, since the federal power will be nothing but the predominance of England. The mode of weakening the federal authority is only too obvious. 'The more there is of the more,' says a profound Spanish proverb, 'the less there is of the less.' The more the number of separate States in the confederacy, the less will be the weight of England, and the greater the relative authority of Ireland. Let England, Scotland, and Wales become separate States, let the Channel Islands and Man, and, if possible, some colonies, be added to the federation, and as the greatness of England dwindles so the independence of Ireland will grow.

Some seven years ago Sir Gavan Duffy predicted that before ten years had elapsed there would be a federation of the Empire.107 Like other prophets he may have antedated the fulfilment of his prediction, but his dictum is the forecast of an experienced politician—it points to a pressing danger. Home Rule for Ireland menaces the dissolution of the United Kingdom, and the unity of the United Kingdom is the necessary condition for maintaining the existence of the British Empire. Home Rule is the first stage to federalism.

But Irish discontent, should it not find satisfaction in a movement for federalism, will naturally take the form of the demand for colonial or for national independence. You cannot play with the spirit of political nationality. The semi-independence of Ireland from England, combined with the undue influence of Ireland in English politics, is certain to produce both unreasonable and reasonable grounds for still further loosening the tie which binds together the two islands. The cry 'Ireland a nation' is one of which no Irishman need be ashamed, and to which North and South alike, irritated by the vexations of a makeshift constitution, are, as I have already insisted, likely enough to rally.

Nor is it certain that Irish Federalists or Irish Nationalists will not obtain allies in England. The politicians who are content with a light heart to destroy the work of Pitt may, for aught I know, with equal levity, annul the Union with Scotland and undo the work of Somers, or by severing Wales from the rest of England render futile the achievement of the greatest of the Plantagenets. Enthusiasts for 'Home Rule all round' would appear to regard their capacity for destroying the United Kingdom as a proof of their ability to build up a new fabric of Imperial power, and to fulfil their vain dreams of a federated Empire. Sensible men may doubt whether a turn for revolutionary destruction is any evidence that politicians possess the rare gift of constructive statesmanship. And should the working of the new constitution confirm these doubts, persons of prudence will begin to perceive that Irish independence is for both England and Ireland a less evil than the extension of federalism.

The natural expression however of English discontent or disappointment is reactionary opposition. Reaction, or the attempt of one party in a state to reverse a fundamental policy deliberately adopted by the nation, is one of the worst among the offspring of revolution, and is almost, though not entirely, unknown to the history of England. Yet there is more than one reason why if the Home Rule Bill be carried, reaction should make its ill-omened appearance in the field of English public life. The policy of Home Rule, even should it be for the moment successful, lacks the moral sanctions which have compelled English statesmen to accept accomplished facts. The methods of agitation in its favour have outraged the moral sense of the community. Mr. Gladstone's victory is the victory of Mr. Parnell, and the triumph of Parnellism is the triumph of conspiracy, and of conspiracy rendered the more base because it was masked under the appearance of a constitutional movement. Neither the numbers nor the composition of the ministerial majority are impressive. The tactics of silence, evasion, and ambiguity may aid in gaining a parliamentary victory, but deprive the victory of that respect for the victors on the part of the vanquished which, in civil contests at any rate, alone secures permanent peace. But the pleas and justifications for reaction are rarely its causes. If Englishmen attempt to bring about the legal destruction of the new constitution, their action will be produced by a sense of the false position assigned to England. No device of statesmanship can stand which is condemned by the nature of things. The predominance of England in the affairs of the United Kingdom is secured by sanctions which in the long run can neither be defied nor set aside; the constitution which does not recognise this predominance is doomed to ruin. That its overthrow would be just no one dare predict; the future is as uncertain as it is dark. A main reason why a wise man must deprecate the weak surrender by Englishmen of rightful power is the dread that, if in a moment of irritation they reassert their strength, they may exhibit neither their good faith nor their justice.

Chapter IV—Pleas For The New Constitution

Gladstonians when pressed with the manifest objections to which the new constitution is open rely for its defence either upon general considerations intended to show that the criticisms on the new constitution are in themselves futile, or upon certain more or less specific arguments, of which the main object is to establish that the policy of Home Rule is either necessary or at least free from danger, and that, therefore, this policy and the new constitution in which it is to be embodied deserve a trial.

My object in this chapter is to examine with fairness the value both of these general considerations and of these specific arguments.

The general considerations are based upon the alleged prophetic character of the criticisms on the new constitution or upon the anomalies to be found in the existing English constitution.

Ministerialists try to invalidate strictures on the Home Rule Bill, such as those set forth in the foregoing pages, by the assertion that the objections are mere prophecy and therefore not worth attention.

This line of defence may, as against Home Rulers, be disposed of at once by an *argumentum ad hominem*. No politicians have made freer use of prediction. Every Gladstonian speech is in effect a statement that is a prophecy of the benefits which Home Rule will confer on the United Kingdom. Gladstonian anticipations no doubt are prophecies of future blessings; but whoever foretells the future is equally a prophet, whether he announces the end of the world or foretells the dawn of a millennium. And history affords no presumption in favour of the prophet who prophesies smooth things. The prognostics of a pessimist may be as much belied by the event as the hopes of an optimist. But for one prophet to decry the predictions of another simply as prophecies is a downright absurdity. Even among rival soothsayers some regard must be had to fairness and common sense; when Zedekiah, the son of Chenaanah, smote Micaiah on the cheek, he struck him not on the ground that he prophesied but that his gloomy predictions were false. Zedekiah was an imposter, he was not a fool, and after all Micaiah, who prophesied evil and not good, turned out the true prophet.

But an *argumentum ad hominem* is never a satisfactory form of reasoning, and it is worth while considering for a moment what is the value of prophecy or foresight in politics. Candour compels the admission that anticipations of the future are at best most uncertain. Cobden and Bright foretold that Free Trade would benefit England; they also foretold that the civilised world would, influenced by England's example, reject protective tariffs. Neither anticipation was unreasonable, but the one was justified whilst the other was confuted by events. All that can be said is that on such anticipations, untrustworthy though they may be, the conduct no less of public than of private life depends. Criticism on anything that is new and untried, whether it be a new-built bridge or a new-made constitution, is of necessity predictive. But there is an essential difference between foresight and guessing. The prevision of a philosophic statesman is grounded on the knowledge of the past and on the analysis of existing tendencies. It deals with principles. Such, for example, was the foresight of Burke when he dogmatically foretold that the French Constitution of 1791 could not stand.108 Guessing is at best based on acute observation of the current events of the day, that is of things which are in their nature uncertain. On January 29, 1848, Tocqueville analysed the condition of French society, and in the Chamber of Deputies foretold the approach of revolution. On February 21, 1848, Girardin said that the monarchy of July would not last three days longer. February 24 verified the insight and foresight of the statesman, and proved that the journalist was an acute observer. The difference is worth consideration. Tocqueville's prophecy would in all probability have been substantially realised had Louis Philippe shown as much energy in 1848 as in 1832, and had the Orleanist dynasty reigned till after his death. Girardin's guess would not have been even a happy hit if one of a thousand accidents had averted the catastrophe of February 24. The worth of the arguments against or for the new constitution depends upon the extent to which they are based upon a mastery of general principles and upon a sound analysis of the conditions of the time, and in these conditions are included the character of the English and of the Irish people. But to object to criticisms simply as prophecies is to reject foresight and to forbid politicians who are creating a constitution for the future to consider what will be its future working.

Another Gladstonian argument is that because the English constitution itself is full of paradoxes, peculiarities, and anomalies, therefore the contradictions or anomalies which are patent in the new constitution (such for example as the retention of the Irish members at Westminster) are of no importance.

The fact asserted is past dispute. Our institutions are based upon fictions. The Prime Minister, the real head of the English Executive, is an official unknown to the law. The Queen, who is the only constitutional head of the Executive, is not the real head of the Government. The Crown possesses a veto on all legislation and never exercises it; the House of Lords might, if the House pleased, reject year by year every Bill sent up to it by the House of Commons; yet such a course of action is never actually pursued and could not be dreamt of except by a madman. There is no advantage in exemplifying further a condition of things which must be known to every person who has the slightest acquaintance with either the law, or the custom, of the constitution. But the inference which Gladstonian apologists draw from the existence of anomalies is, in the strict sense of the word, preposterous. On the face of the matter it is a strange way of reasoning to say that because the constitution is filled with odd arrangements which no man can justify in theory, you therefore, when designing a new constitution, should take no care to make your arrangements consistent and harmonious. But the Gladstonian error goes a good deal deeper than is at first sight apparent. The anomalies or the fictions of the constitution are in reality adaptations, often awkward enough in themselves, of some old institution, and are preserved because, though they look strange, they are found to work well. Thus the King of England was at one time the actual sovereign of the State, or at any rate the most important member of the sovereign power, and the Ministers were in reality, what they are still in name, the King's servants. The powers of the Crown have been greatly diminished, and have been transferred in effect to the Houses of Parliament, or rather to the House of Commons, and the Ministers taken from the Houses are in fact, though not in name, servants of Parliament. This arrangement leaves an undefined and undefinable amount of authority to the Crown. It is not an arrangement which any man would have planned beforehand; but it is kept up, not because it is an anomaly, but because it has, as a matter of experience, turned out convenient. What even plausible argument can thence be drawn to show that a new constitutional arrangement, on the face of it awkward and inconvenient, will for some unknown reason turn out workable and beneficial? He who reasons thus, if reasoning it can be called, might as well argue that because an old shoe which has gradually been worn to the form of the foot is comfortable, therefore a shoemaker need not care to make a new shoe fit.

These two general replies to strictures on the new constitution are in themselves of no worth whatever. They deserve examination for two reasons only. They are, in various shapes, put forward by politicians of eminence, they exhibit further in a clear form a defect which mars a good deal of Gladstonian reasoning. Ministerialists seem to think that arguments good for the purpose of conservatism are available for the purpose of innovation. This is an error. A conservative reasoner may urge the uncertainty of all prevision, or the fact that the actual constitution, though theoretically absurd or imperfect, works well, as reasons of some weight, though not of overwhelming weight, for leaving things as they are, but it must puzzle any sensible man to see how either the uncertainty of prevision or the fair working of existing institutions can be twisted into reasons for taking a political leap in the dark.

Let us dismiss then objections which as they are fatal to all criticism are in reality ineffective against any criticism of our new constitution. When this is done it will be found that the Gladstonian pleas in favour of Home Rule, for such are in reality their apologies for the new constitution, may be brought under two heads. They are intended to show, first, that the concession of parliamentary independence to Ireland is a necessity, and, secondly, that at worst it involves no danger.109

A. *Necessity for Home Rule.*

That the concession of Home Rule to Ireland is a necessity, forms the implied, if not always the asserted, foundation of the case in favour of Gladstonian policy.

Ireland, it is argued, has for generations been discontented and disloyal. Every sort of remedy has been tried. The rule of the ordinary law, coercion, Protestant supremacy, Catholic relief, the disestablishment of the Anglican Church, the maintenance of the English land tenure and English landlordism, the introduction of a new system of land tenure unknown to any other country in the world and more favourable to tenants than the land law of any other State in Europe, the removal of every grievance which could be made patent to the Imperial Parliament, every plan or experiment which could approve itself to the judgment of English politicians has been tried, and no scheme, however plausible, has ended in success. Concession has proved as useless as severity, and the existence in the Statute Book of a permanent Coercion Act is a standing proof of failure. He who asserts that Irish disloyalty or discontent has not declined understates the case. It has increased. Grattan was a statesman of a more exalted type than O'Connell, and Grattan was more zealous for connection with England than was the Roman Catholic tribune. And though in Grattan's time the grievances of Ireland were in every man's judgment far more intolerable than, even on the showing of Home Rulers, are the wrongs which Ireland now endures, the Ireland of Grattan was loyal to England. O'Connell was a nobler leader than Parnell, and it would be absurd to suppose that any Parnellite or Anti-Parnellite exerted a tenth of O'Connell's influence. Yet Parnell and Parnell's followers have achieved a feat which the hero of Catholic emancipation could never accomplish; O'Connell never obtained for Repeal more than half the votes of Ireland's parliamentary representatives; Parnell and his followers have rallied the vast majority of Irish members in support of Home Rule. Meanwhile year by year the government of England is weakened, and (though the argument comes awkwardly from the mouth of English constitutionalists who are allies and friends of conspirators and boycotters) the morality of English public life has been undermined, by the presence at Westminster of Irish members who, regarding the English Parliament as an alien power, weaken its action, despise its traditions, and degrade its character. One remedy for Irish miseries and for English dangers has not been tried. No English statesman before Mr. Gladstone (it is urged) has offered to Ireland the one thing which Ireland desires—the boon or right of parliamentary independence. Be the desire for Home Rule reasonable or not, it is Home Rule for which Ireland longs. Ireland feels herself a nation. Satisfy then Ireland's wish, meet the feeling of nationality, and Ireland will be at rest. This experiment must at least be tried; its perils must be risked. The present situation is intolerable, the concession of Home Rule to Ireland is a necessity.

This, to the best of my apprehension, is the Gladstonian argument. My aim has certainly been to state it fairly and in its full force.

Is the argument valid? Is the plea of necessity made out? The answer may be given without hesitation. It is not. The allegations on which the whole train of reasoning rests are tainted by exaggeration or misapprehension, and the allegations, even if taken as true, do not establish the required inference; the premises are unsound, and the premises do not support the conclusion.

The premises are unsound.

The Gladstonians are far too much of parliamentary formalists. Their imagination and their reason are impressed by the strength in the House of Commons of the Irish party. The eighty votes from Ireland daunt them. But wise men must look behind votes at facts. The eighty Irish Home Rulers are, it is true, no light matter, even when allowance is made for the way in which corruption and intimidation vitiate the vote of Ireland. But their voice is not the voice of the Irish people; it is at most the mutter or the clamour of a predominant Irish faction. It is the voice of Ireland in the same sense in which a century ago the shouts or yells of the Jacobin Club were the voice of France. To any one who looks behind the forms of the constitution to the realities of life, the voice of Irish wealth, of Irish intelligence, and of Irish loyalty is at least as important as the voice of Irish sedition or discontent. The eighty votes must in any case be reckoned morally at not more than sixty, for to this number they would be reduced by any fair and democratic scheme of representation. No one can be less tempted than myself to make light of Irish turbulence and Irish misery. But it must not be exaggerated. The discontent of 1893 is nothing to the rebellion, sedition, or disloyalty of 1782, of 1798, of 1829, or of 1848. If Irishmen of one class are discontented, Irishmen of another class are contented, prosperous, and loyal. The protest of Irish Protestants—the grandsons of the men who detested the Union—against the dissolution of the Union, is the reward and triumph of Pitt's policy of Union.

The eighty Irish members ask for Home Rule, but the tenant farmers of Ireland ask not for Home Rule but for the ownership of the land; and the Irish tenant farmers will and may under a Unionist Government become owners of their land, and, what is no slight matter, may become owners by honest means. Vain for Mr. M'Carthy110 to assert that Irish farmers would not have accepted even from Mr. Parnell the most favourable of land laws in exchange for Home Rule. Mr. M'Carthy believes what he says, but it is impossible for any student of Irish history or of Irish politics to believe Mr. M'Carthy. Facts are too strong for him. Mr. Lalor showed a prevision denied to our amiable novelist. Gustave de Beaumont understood political philosophy better than the lively recorder of the superficial aspects of recent English history. Mr. Parnell and Mr. Davitt, and the whole line of witnesses before the Special Commission, tell a different tale. The very name of the *Land* League is significant. Home Rule was a mere theme for academic discussion in the mouth of Mr. Butt. Repeal itself never touched the strongest passions of Irish nature, though advocated by the most eloquent and popular of Irish orators. Not an independent Parliament, but independent ownership of land, has always been the desire of Irish cultivators. It was a cry for the land which gave force to the demand for Home Rule; and an Irish agitator, if his strength fails, renews it by touching the earth. But why confine our observation to Ireland? We here come upon the passions, not of Irish nature, but of human nature. There is not a landowner in France who does not care tenfold more for the security of his land than for the form of the government. If peasants trembled for their property the Republic would fall to-morrow. This is no mere conjecture; the peasantry were Jacobins as long as the Jacobins gave them the land, they were Imperialists whilst Napoleon was their security against a restoration which to them meant confiscation of land purchased or seized during the Revolution. The country population of France heard with indifference of the fall of Louis Philippe, and possibly approved the proclamation of the second Republic. But the communism of 1848 roused every landowner against Paris. The peasant proprietors filled the benches of the National Assembly with Conservatives or Reactionists who would save them from plunder; fear became for once the cause of courage, and dread of loss of property sent thousands of peasant proprietors to Paris, that they might crush by force of arms the socialist insurrection of June. Perjury, fraud, and cruelty disgraced the *coup d'état* of 1851. But, as Liberals now see, the second Empire, hateful though it was to every man who loved freedom or cared for integrity, did not owe the permanence of its power to cunning or to violence. It was the dread of the Red Spectre which drove the landowners of France into Imperialism; they may have liked parliamentary liberty, it was a pleasant luxury, but they loved their land and property, it was their life-blood, and by Socialism their land and property was they believed menaced.

As to the Coercion Act, no sensible man, be he Radical or Tory, need trouble himself. The Criminal Law and Procedure (Ireland) Act, 1887, is neither a disgrace to England nor an injury to Ireland. Its permanence, which is the cause of its mildness, is its merit. Well would it have been had the Act been extended to the whole United Kingdom. Local laws are open to some of the same objections as temporary laws. The enactment contains some improvements in our criminal procedure. There is no more idle superstition than the belief that criminal procedure does not, like other human arrangements, require change. If incendiarism should become an element in the conduct of trade disputes, if dynamite is to be recognised as a legitimate arm in political conflicts, the criminal law of the United Kingdom will, we may be sure, need and receive several alterations and improvements.

By far the strongest portion of the Gladstonian argument is the stress that can be laid on the demoralisation of Parliament, produced partly, though not wholly, by the Irish vote. This is a consideration which, as far as it goes, tells in favour of Home Rule. It is, however, a consideration of which the Gladstonian apologist for the new constitution of 1893 [can] make no use. His reasoning of necessity stands thus:

The presence of 80 Irish members at Westminster has demoralised Parliament, therefore we must above all things retain 80 or possibly 103 Irish members at Westminster. He is placed in a hopeless dilemma; he dare not draw the only conclusion to which his argument points, namely, that the Irish members must be excluded from the Parliament at Westminster. By a strange fatality, the policy of 1823 retrospectively condemns the policy of 1886, whilst the very strongest argument in favour of the policy of 1886 condemns the policy of 1893.

The premises, were they sound, do not support the conclusion.

There exists undoubtedly such a thing in politics as necessity.

When England acknowledged the independence of the Thirteen Colonies, or when France surrendered Metz and Strasburg, no one could talk of imprudence of impolicy. The will of Englishmen and of Frenchmen was coerced by the force of events. When all Protestant Ireland was in arms, when the whole Irish nation demanded parliamentary independence, when England had been defeated in America, when France and Spain were allied against her, then the acceptance of Grattan's declaration of right was in truth a necessity. When Wellington became the supporter of Catholic Emancipation because he would not face civil war, when famine was at our gates and Peel repealed the corn laws—then again politicians could plead the excuse of necessity. In these and like crises the wisest men and the bravest men are forced to recognise the logic of facts; and necessity rather than prudence dictates the courseof statesmanship. But no such crisis has now arisen. England and Ireland were as safe under the government of Lord Salisbury as under the government of Mr. Gladstone—perhaps safer. No one except an extremely excited and very rhetorical politician will venture to assert that, if Lord Salisbury instead of Mr. Gladstone had last summer gained a majority of forty, any man or woman throughout the United Kingdom would have trembled for the safety of the country. The sky is far less dark than on that fearful day eleven years back111 when England stood aghast at the assassinations of the Phoenix Park. Irish discontent is an immense evil, of which every just man must deplore the existence; its removal would be the greatest benefit which statesmanship could by any possibility confer upon England. But the immediate dealing with it in a particular way is not a necessity. Were the Home Rule Bill, and every Home Rule Bill, rejected by Parliament, the United Kingdom would be as safe as it has been at any time for the last ninety years and more.

In plain truth we have all of us forgotten the meaning of necessity. Gladstonians have come honestly to confuse the needs of a party with the necessities of the country. This is a delusion that at all times and in all lands affects great political connections which, having once rendered high services to the nation, have outlived the valid reasons for their existence. The Republicans saved the United States from disruption. Hence in 1888, when Secession was an historical memory, many of the most to be respected among Americans believed that the rule of an honest Democrat was a worse evil than the rule of a corrupt Republican. Thousands of Frenchmen, amidst the moral bankruptcy of Republican politicians, still hold that, because Republicans years ago saved France from ruin, even reconciled Conservatives cannot in the year 1893 be placed in office without danger to the commonwealth. So it is abroad; so it has been in England. In 1760 the best and wisest of English statesmen deemed it impossible that England should be rightly governed by any politicians but the representatives of the Revolution Families. In 1829 honest citizens trembled at the thought of power passing into the hands of the Whigs; for the Tories had ruled for nearly sixty years, and the Tories had preserved England from revolution and invasion. So at this moment to many well-meaning Liberals the long predominance of the Liberal party makes the possibility of a Cabinet containing politicians who may in any sense be called Tories seem a monstrous calamity, which it is a necessity to avert. Vain to point out that Lord Salisbury and Mr. Balfour are such Tories as Eldon would have called Jacobins and Lord Melbourne Radicals, and that, they are allied with the best and most trustworthy of living Liberal leaders. Their is no arguing with sentiment; it is necessary to keep the Gladstonian Liberals in office, and the constitution must be sacrificed in order that Lord Salisbury may not resume the Premiership. But there is a deeper cause than all this for our strange ideas of necessity. Habitual ease and unvarying prosperity have for a moment lowered the national spirit. Englishmen confuse inconveniences with dangers; they have forgotten what real peril is; they cannot understand the calmness with which, not a century ago, their fathers resisted at once insurrection in Ireland and the most powerful foreign enemy who has ever challenged the power of England, and this too at a time when the population of Great Britain was not above nine millions and the people of Ireland numbered more than four millions, when France was the leading military power of the world, and Ireland might at any moment receive the aid of a French army led by one of the best French generals. The men of 1798 or 1800 would mock at our ideas of necessity. Ireland has not an eighth of the population of the United Kingdom; our Home Rulers are not Ireland; they are a very different thing—the Irish populace. Let us yield everything which ought to be yielded to justice; let us obey the dictates of expediency, which is only justice looked at from another side; let us concede much to generosity; but in the name of common sense, of honesty, and of manliness, let us hear no more of necessity. Once in an age necessity may be the defence of statesmanship forced to confess its own blindness, but it is far more often the plea of tyranny, of ambition, of cowardice, or despair.

B. *No danger in Home Rule.*

The arguments which are employed to show that the policy of Home Rule and the new constitution which embodies it involve no danger for England are in the main drawn from the 'Safeguards' or Restrictions contained in the Bill— from the alleged precedent of Grattan's Constitution—from the success of Home Rule in other parts of the world—and, generally, from the expediency of trustfulness.

i. *The Safeguards.*

The Restrictions on the power of the Irish Parliament are, it is asserted, sufficient and more than sufficient to reassure Unionists, and an intimation is sometimes added that, if further security is wanted, further safeguards may be provided.

This ground of confidence may be briefly dismissed; its answer is in effect supplied by the foregoing pages.

On the action of the Irish Executive the Restrictions place, and from the nature of things can place, no restraint whatever, and yet both England and the Irish Loyalists have far more reason to dread the abuse of executive than of legislative authority. On the legal action of the Irish Parliament the Restrictions do place a certain restraint, but the Restrictions are, as already shown, not in reality enforceable. They are for good purposes a nullity; they are effective, if at all, almost wholly for evil; they exhibit the radical and fatal inconsistency of Gladstonian policy. The policy of Home Rule is a policy of absolute and unrestricted trust; the safeguards are based on distrust. There is something to be said for generous confidence, and something also for distrustful prudence; there is nothing to be said for ineffective suspicion.

ii. *Grattan's Constitution.*

From the asserted harmony between England and Ireland from 1782 to 1800 under Grattan's Constitution, the inference is drawn that there is no reason to fear discord between England and Ireland under the Gladstonian constitution of 1893.

The fallacy underlying the appeal to this precedent has been, to use words of Mr. Lecky, 'so frequently exposed that I can only wonder at its repetition.' 112 Under Grattan's Constitution the Irish Executive was appointed, not by the Irish Parliament, but by the English Ministry; the Irish Parliament consisted solely of Protestants; it represented the miscalled 'English garrison,' and was in sympathy with the governing classes of England. With all this to promote harmony, the concord between the governing powers in England and in Ireland was dubious. The rejection of England's proposals as to trade, and the exaction of the Renunciation Act, betray a condition of opinion which at any moment might have produced open discord. When at last the parliamentary independence of Ireland had led up to a savage rebellion, suppressed I fear with savage severity, English statesmen knew that an independent Irish Parliament threatened the existence of England. I may be allowed, even by Gladstonians, to place the genius and patriotism of Pitt on at least a level with the genius and patriotism of the present Premier. I may be allowed to doubt whether Mr. Gladstone's studies, however profound, in the history of Ireland, can, in 1893, render his acquaintance with the circumstances and the dangers of 1800 equal to the knowledge of the Minister who, in 1800, carried the Act of Union. And Pitt then held that the Union with Ireland was necessary for the preservation of England. If moreover Grattan's Constitution be a precedent for our guidance, let us see to what the precedent points. The leading principles or features of Grattan's Constitution are well known. They are the absolute sovereignty of the Irish Parliament, and its independence of and equality with the Parliament of Great Britain; the renunciation by the British Parliament of any claim whatever to legislate for Ireland, and of any jurisdiction on the part of any British court to entertain appeals from Ireland;

and, lastly, the absence of all representation of Ireland in the Parliament at Westminster. Each of these principles or features is denied or reversed by our new Gladstonian constitution. The Irish Parliament is to be, not a sovereign legislature, but a subordinate legislature created by statute, and a legislature of such restricted and inferior authority as to be unworthy of the name of a parliament. The Imperial Parliament, with its vast majority of British members, asserts its absolute supremacy in Ireland, and the right at its discretion to legislate for Ireland on any matter whatever; in Ireland there is to be founded an Imperial or British Court appointed by the Imperial Ministry, having jurisdiction on all matters affecting Imperial rights, and the final Court of Appeal from every tribunal in Ireland is to be the British Privy Council. Add to this that Irish members are to sit in the Parliament of Westminster as the 'outward and visible sign' of the Imperial Parliament's supremacy. But if every principle of Grattan's Constitution be contradicted by the Gladstonian constitution, if every principle which Grattan detested is a principle which Mr. Gladstone asserts, with what show of reason can the success, uncertain though it be, of the Constitution of 1782 be pleaded as evidence of the probable success of the Gladstonian constitution of 1893? That two arrangements are unlike is to ordinary minds no proof that they will have similar results; a parliamentary majority of forty-two may repeal the Act of Union, but it cannot repeal the laws of logic.113

iii. *Success of Home Rule.*

All over the world, we are told, Home Rule has succeeded; there are, under the government of the British Crown, at least twenty countries enjoying Home Rule, and their local independence causes no inconvenience to the United Kingdom or to the British Empire. It follows therefore that Home Rule in Ireland will be a success and will in no way disturb the peace or prosperity of the United Kingdom.

The sole difficulty in meeting this argument is the extreme vagueness of its principal term. The words 'Home Rule' are in their signification so vague, at any rate as employed by Ministerialists, that they cover governments of totally different descriptions. Hungary, Norway, a State of the American Union, a Province of the Canadian Dominion, the Dominion itself, Man, Jersey, and Guernsey, every English colony with representative institutions, are each described, by one Gladstonian reasoner or another, as happy and prosperous under Home Rule. But there is no one who will deny that the dissimilarities between the governments existing in each of the countries referred to are at least as striking as are their similarities; that the contrast, for example, between the relation of Hungary to the Austro-Hungarian Empire and the relation of New York to the United States is at least as obvious as its likeness. The analogy, moreover, between Home Rule in any of these countries and Home Rule in Ireland is at best distant and shadowy.114

The crisis is too serious to permit us to waste words in examining the curiosities of the Home Rule controversy. Of Hungary, and its relation to the Empire of which it forms part, nothing at all will here be said. There is nothing in that relation analogous to Irish Home Rule. Nor need we trouble ourselves with the 'Home Rule' of Rhodes, of Samos, or of the Lebanon. Of these and any other States, if such there be, which enjoy 'Home Rule' under the supremacy of the Sultan, all that need be said is that it is satisfactory to learn on the authority of Mr. Gladstone that any part whatever of the Turkish Empire is well governed and happy. If any one can seriously suppose that the prosperity of Man and the Channel Islands, which reap all the benefits and bear none of the burdens of connection with Great Britain, and moreover have at no time been discontented, affords any reason for supposing that the secular miseries and discontent of Ireland will be cured by a system of government totally different from that which prevails either in Man, or Guernsey, or in Jersey, let him refer to these interesting islands.115 For myself I shall leave them out of account. Of the cordial relations between Sweden and Norway we hear nothing; the goodwill generated by a system of Home Rule is bringing these countries to the brink of civil war.116

There are two analogous cases or precedents on which serious reasoners rely in support of a policy of Home Rule for Ireland. The success of federal government in other countries, and especially in the United States, and the success of colonial independence throughout the British Empire, are adduced as presumptions that Home Rule would knit together Great Britain and Ireland, or, as the cant of the day goes, transform a paper union into a union of hearts. If New York be loyal to the United States, if New Zealand be loyal to the British Crown, why should not Ireland, when endowed with local independence resembling the independence of an American State or of a self-governing British colony, be a loyal member of the United Kingdom?117

This is the suggested argument—let us consider its validity.

As to federalism.—All the conditions which make a federal constitution work successfully in the United States, in Switzerland, and possibly in Germany, are wanting in England and Ireland. No man till the last five or six years has even suggested that Englishmen or Scotsmen desire a federal government for its own sake. Whether Mr. Gladstone himself has any wish to federalise the whole United Kingdom is at least open to doubt. Where federalism has succeeded, it has succeeded as a means of uniting separate communities into a nation; it has not been used as a means of disuniting one State into separate nationalities. The United States, it has been well said, is a nation under the form of a federal government. Gladstonians apparently wish to bind together two, or shall we say three or four, nations, or nationalities, under the reality of a federation and the name of a United Kingdom. While all the powerful countries of the world are increasing their strength by union, the advocates of the new constitution pretend to increase the moral strength of the United Kingdom by loosening the ties of its political unity. If any one ask why federalism which has succeeded in America should not succeed in the United Kingdom, the true answer is best suggested by another question: Why would not the constitutional monarchy of England suit the United States? The answer in each case is the same. The circumstances and wants of the two countries are essentially different; and if this be not a sufficient reply, the reflection is worth making that in the three great Confederacies of the world unity has been achieved, or enforced by armed conflict.

As to colonial independence.—The plain and decisive reason why the loyalty of New Zealand to the Empire affords no presumption of the loyalty under our new constitution of Ireland to the United Kingdom is this: The whole condition of New Zealand is different from the condition of Ireland, and our new constitution is not intended to give Ireland the position of New Zealand. Thousands of miles separate New Zealand from Great Britain. Ireland is separated from us by not much more than twelve miles. New Zealand has never been hostile to England; her people are loyal to the British Crown. Ireland, or part of the Irish people, has been divided from England by a feud of centuries; it would be difficult among Irish Nationalists to obtain even the show of loyalty to the Crown. New Zealand is wealthy, and New Zealand pays not a single tax into the Exchequer of the United Kingdom. Ireland is poor, and, if her taxation is lightened by Home Rule, the tribute which will be paid to England will be heavy, and far more galling than the taxes she now pays in common with the rest of the United Kingdom. The new constitution, again, is utterly unlike a colonial constitution. Its burdens would not be tolerated by any one of our independent colonies. The rights it gives, no less than the obligations it imposes, are foreign to our colonial system. The presence of the Irish representation at Westminster forbids all comparison between Ireland under Home Rule and New Zealand under a system of colonial independence.

But the matter must be pressed further. Even were it possible to place Ireland in the position either of an American State or Swiss Canton, or of an independent colony, the arrangement would not meet the needs of the United Kingdom. This is a point which has not as yet arrested attention. For the safety of the United Kingdom it is absolutely necessary that the authority of the Imperial Government, or, in other words, the law of the land, should be enforced in Ireland in a sense in which the law of the land is rarely enforced in federations, and in which it is certainly not enforced by the Imperial Government in self-governing colonies.

In federations the law of the land is nearly powerless when opposed to the will of a particular State. President Jackson's reported dictum, 'John Marshall118 has delivered his judgment, let him now enforce it if he can,' and the fact that the judgment was never enforced,119 are things not to be forgotten. They are worth a thousand disquisitions on the admirable working of federalism. But there is no need to rely on a traditional story, which, however, is an embodiment of an undoubted transaction. The plainest facts of American history all tell the same tale. No Abolitionist could in 1850 without peril to his life have preached abolition in South Carolina; difficult indeed was the enforcement of the Fugitive Slave Law and small the practical respect paid in Massachusetts to the doctrine of the Dred Scott Case. Unless all reports are false, the Negro vote throughout the Southern States is at this moment practically falsified, and little do the Constitutional Amendments benefit a Negro in any case where his conduct offends Southern principle or prejudice. For my present argument it matters nothing whether the oppression of individuals or the defiance of law was or was not, in all these cases, as it certainly was in some instances, a violation to the supreme law of the land. If the law was violated then, why should we expect Imperial law to be of more force in Ireland than federal law in South Carolina, or in Massachusetts? If the rights of individuals were not adequately protected by federal law against the injustice of a particular State, then why expect that the provisions of our new constitution, far less stringent as they are than the protective provisions of the United States Constitution, should avail to protect unpopular persons in Ireland against the legal tyranny of the Irish Executive or the Irish Parliament?

Experience of federalism is not confined to the United States. The Swiss Confederation is in Europe the most successful both of democratic and of federal polities. The Swiss Executive exercises powers common to all continental governments but of a description which no English Cabinet could claim, and the Swiss Executive is made up of statesmen skilful beyond measure in what may be called the diplomacy of federalism. Yet in Switzerland, as in the United States, federal government means weak government. Ticino is a small Canton, but from the days of Athenian greatness small States have been the instructors of the world, and Englishmen, hesitating over a political leap in the dark, would do well to study the Ticinese revolution of September 11, 1890. The Radicals of the Canton rose in insurrection, and deposed the lawful government by violence; as Englishmen may remember, the contest though short involved at least one murder. The

Swiss Executive (called the Federal Council) forthwith took steps to restore order and to reinstate the lawful Cantonal government. Their own commissioner, a military officer, in effect declined to put the overthrown government back in power. Order was restored, but the law was never vindicated. A strange set of negotiations, transactions, or intrigues took place. In the Federal Assembly at Berne, the Conservatives, a minority, urged the rights of the lawful government of Ticino. The Liberals defended or palliated the revolutionists. On the whole the advantage seems to have rested with the latter. A trial before a Federal Court took place, but the accused were acquitted. No one, if I am rightly informed, was punished for an act of manifest treason. It is even more noticeable that Professor Hilty, a distinguished and respected Swiss publicist, vindicates or palliates the admitted breach of law, in deference to the principle or sentiment, which if true has wide application, that 'human nature is not revolutionary, and that no revolution ever arises without a heavy share of guilt (Mitschuld) on the part of the government against which the revolution is directed.' 120 The instructiveness of this passage in Swiss history as regards the working of our new constitution is obvious; Englishmen should specially note the interconnection between lawlessness in Ticino and the balance of parties at Berne; it is easy to foresee an analogous connection between revolution, say in Dublin or Belfast, and the balance of parties at Westminster. But this is not my immediate point; my point is that the Federal Government at Berne cannot enforce obedience to law in Ticino in the way in which Englishmen expect that the Imperial Government shall, under any circumstances, enforce or cause the law to be enforced in Ireland.

But Ireland, it will be said, is to occupy a position like that of a self-governing colony. In British colonies the Imperial power and the rule of law are respected; both therefore will be respected in Ireland. The plain answer to this suggestion is that in a British self-governing colony, no law is enforceable which is opposed to colonial sentiment and which the colonial Ministry refuse to put into execution. One well-ascertained fact is enough to dispose of a hundred platitudes about Imperial supremacy and the loyal obedience of our colonies. Victoria is as loyal to the Crown as any colony which England possesses, yet the submission to law of the Victorian Government and people is not by any means unlimited. Ten years ago three British subjects arrived at Melbourne and were about to land. Popular sentiment, or in other words the will of the mob, had decreed that they should not enter the colony. The Victorian Premier (Mr. Service) announced in Parliament that their landing should be hindered. The police, acting under the orders of the Ministry, boarded the ship which brought the strangers, went near to assaulting the captain, and forcibly prevented the hated travellers from setting foot on shore.

By arrangement between the Melbourne Government, the captain, and the three men, who were by this time in terror of their lives, the victims of lawlessness were carried back to England. That the law had been grossly violated no one can really dispute. The violation was the more serious because it excited no notice. No appeal was apparently made to the Courts. The Governor—the representative of Imperial power and Imperial justice—knew presumably what was going on, yet he uttered not one word of remonstrance. The Agent-General for Victoria, when at last a private person in England called attention to the outrage at Melbourne, pleaded in effect the plea of necessity, and described the act of tyranny, whereby British citizens were in a British colony turned into outlaws, as 'an act of executive authority.' The Imperial Government did I believe—what was perhaps the wisest thing it could do—nothing. Imperial supremacy in the colonies was, as regards the protection of unpopular individuals, admitted to be a farce. What, however, rendered the three travellers unpopular? They were Irish informers who had aided, unless I am mistaken, in the conviction of the Phoenix Park murderers. Let us now in imagination conceive our new constitution to have come into being, and transfer the transactions at Melbourne in 1883 to Dublin in 1894. Will the Imperial supremacy which is supposed to be so effective in the colonies be of any more worth in Ireland than in Victoria?121

Were it true, then, which it certainly is not, that the conditions exist in Ireland which conduce to the maintenance of federal power in the State of a well-arranged federation, and to the maintenance of Imperial power in a self-governing British colony, this would not be enough to support the argument in favour of the new constitution. For the Imperial Government needs that the law should be maintained, and the rights of individuals be protected, in Ireland with greater stringency than the law is enforced or the rights of individuals are protected either under a federal government or in a British colony. Miserable indeed would be the position of England were she forced in Ireland to wink at lawlessness such as but the other day disgraced New Orleans, or at mob law countenanced by the 'Executive,' such as in 1883 ruled supreme at Melbourne. Foreign powers at any rate would rightly decline to let the defects of our constitution excuse the neglect of international duties. If England cannot shuffle off her responsibilities, England is bound in prudence to maintain her power.

iv. *The Policy of Trust.*

'I believe myself that suspicion is the besetting vice of politicians and that trust is often the truest wisdom.'122

This sentiment is followed by curious and ambiguous qualifications. It is not cited for the sake of fixing Mr. Gladstone with any doctrine whatever; it is quoted because it neatly expresses the sentiment which, in one form or another, underlies most of the arguments in favour of Home Rule or of our new constitution. The right attitude for a politician, it is urged, is trust; he should trust the Irish leaders and their assurances or professions; he should trust in the training conferred upon men by the exercise of power; he should trust in the healing effects of a policy of conciliation, or, to put the matter shortly, he should trust in the goodness and reasonableness of human nature. Exercise only a little trustfulness and the policy of Home Rule, it is suggested, may be seen to be a wise and prudent policy.[123]

How far, then, is trust in any of the three forms, which it may on this occasion take, a reasonable sentiment?

We are told to trust the Irish leaders.

My answer to this advice is plain and decided. Confidence is not a matter of choice. You cannot give your trust simply because you wish to give it. Men are trusted because they are trustworthy. The Irish Home Rule leaders as a body cannot inspire trust, for the simple reason that their whole policy and conduct prove them untrustworthy. Politicians, strange as the fact may appear to them, cannot get quit of their past.

Look for a moment at the history—the patent, acknowledged history—of the agitators or the patriots (and I doubt not that many of them are, from their own point of view, patriotic) in whom we are asked to confide, and whose assurances are to form the basis on which to rest a dubious policy. They have been till recently the foes of England. This in itself is not much; many a rebel has been the enemy of England, and yet has been entitled to the respect of Englishmen. But there are deeds which neither hatred to England nor love of Ireland can justify. Even sedition has its moral code, and like war itself is subject to obligations which no man can neglect without infamy. The conspirators condemned by the Special Commission—and among them are to be found the most prominent of the Irish leaders[124]—have been guilty of conduct which no wise man ought to forget and no good man ought to palliate. They have for years excited Irish ignorance against England and against English officials by a system of gross incessant slander; witness the pages of *United Ireland* when Lord Spencer and Sir George Trevelyan were in power at Dublin. The men whom we are told to trust are men who did enter into a criminal conspiracy by a system of coercion and intimidation to promote an agrarian agitation against the payment of agricultural rents, for the purpose of impoverishing and expelling from the country the English landlords[125]; they are men found guilty of not denouncing intimidation which led to crime and outrage, but of persisting in it with a knowledge of its effect.126 They are proved to have made payments to compensate persons injured in the commission of crime127; they are men who have solicited and taken the money of Patrick Ford, the advocate of dynamite; and have invited and obtained the co-operation of the Clan-na-Gael.128 Their whole system of agitation has been utterly unlike that of honourable agitators, conspirators, or rebels; it would have excited the horror of O'Connell; it would have been repudiated with disgust by Davis, by Gavan Duffy, by Smith O'Brien, and the other Irish leaders of 1848. The men who now ask for our confidence have in their attack upon England forgotten what was due to Ireland; they have deliberately taught Irish peasants lessons of dishonesty, oppression, and cruelty, which the farmers of Ireland may take years to unlearn. Of the degradation which they have gradually inflicted upon the English Parliament one is glad to say little. It is, however, well that the House of Commons should recollect that parliamentary debates are open to all the world and that Englishmen and Englishwomen see no reason why brutalities of expression should be tolerated in the oldest representative Assembly of Europe which would be reproved in any respectable English meeting. But you can sometimes trust men's capacity where you cannot trust their moral feeling. Unfortunately the Irish Parliamentary party have given us examples of their ability in matters of government which are not reassuring. The scenes of Committee Room No. 15129 are a rehearsal of parliamentary life under Home Rule at Dublin.

But the Gladstonians, we shall be told, guarantee the good faith of their associates. Unfortunately, as judges of character the Gladstonians are out of court. The leader who first obtained their confidence was Mr. Parnell. If the Home Rule Bill of 1886 had become law Mr. Parnell would have become Premier of Ireland, and we should have been bidden to put trust in his loyalty and his integrity. There are no Gladstonians now who think Mr. Parnell trustworthy. Why should they be better judges of the trustworthiness of Mr. Dillon, Mr. M'Carthy, or Mr. Davitt, than they were of the character of the statesman who was the leader, friend or patron of the whole Irish Parliamentary party? Note, however—for in this matter it is essential to make one's meaning perfectly clear—I do not allege, or suppose, that the assurances of the Irish leaders are mendacious. They believe, I doubt not, what they say at the moment; but their words mean very little. In a sense they believed, or did not disbelieve, the slanderous accusations which filled the pages of *United Ireland*. In a sense they now believe that the Home Rule Bill is a satisfactory compromise. But the belief in each case must be considered essentially superficial. Men are the victims of their own career: it is absolutely impossible that leaders many of whom have indulged in virulence, in slanders, in cruelty, in oppression, should be suddenly credited with strict truthfulness, with sobriety, with respect for the rights of others. Even as it is, landlords are, in Mr. Sexton's eyes, criminals,130 and he therefore cannot be trusted to act with fairness towards Irish landowners. Mr. Redmond holds that imprisoned dynamiters and other criminals should be released, whether guilty or not, and it is therefore reasonable not to put Mr. Redmond in a position where he can insist upon an amnesty for dynamiters and conspirators. Nor is it at all clear that as regards amnesty any Anti-Parnellite dare dissent from the doctrine of Mr. Redmond. It is odious, it will be said, to dwell on faults or crimes which, were it possible, every man would wish forgotten. But when we are asked to trust politicians who are untrustworthy, it is a duty to say why we must refuse to them every kind of confidence. Of the penalty for such plain speaking I am well aware. It will be said that to attack the Irish leaders is to slander the Irish people. This is untrue. In times of revolution men perpetually come to the front unworthy of the nation whom they lead. To treat distrust of the leaders of the Land League as dislike or distrust of the Irish people is as unfair as to say that the censor of Robespierre, of Marat, or of Barère denies that during the Revolution Frenchmen displayed high genius and rare virtues. There are thousands of Irishmen who will endorse every word I have written about the Irish leaders. Add to this that I am not called upon to pronounce any further condemnation upon the party than was pronounced upon the chief among them by the Special Commission. All I assert is that from the nature of things the men found guilty by the Commission cannot inspire trust.

Power, it is often intimated, teaches its own lessons. Trust Irishmen with the government of their own country, and you may feel confident that experience will teach them how to govern justly.

To this argument I need not myself provide a reply: it has been admirably given by my friend Mr. Bryce. Every word which in the following passage refers to the State legislatures of the United States applies in principle to the future Parliament at Dublin:—

'The chief lesson which a study of the more vicious among the State legislatures teaches, is that power does not necessarily bring responsibility in its train. I should be ashamed to write down so bald a platitude were it not that it is one of those platitudes which are constantly forgotten or ignored. People who know well enough that, in private life, wealth or rank or any other kind of power is as likely to mar a man as to make him, to lower as to raise his sense of duty, have nevertheless contracted the habit of talking as if human nature changed when it entered public life, as if the mere possession of public functions, whether of voting or of legislating, tended of itself to secure their proper exercise. We know that power does not purify men in despotic governments, but we talk as if it did so in free governments. Every one would of course admit, if the point were put flatly to him, that power alone is not enough, but that there must be added to power, in the case of the voter, a direct interest in the choice of good men, in the case of the legislator, responsibility to the voters, in the case of both, a measure of enlightenment and honour. What the legislatures of the worst States show is not merely the need for the existence of a sound public opinion, for such a public opinion exists, but the need for methods by which it can be brought into efficient action upon representatives who, if they are left to themselves, and are not individually persons with a sense of honour and a character to lose, will be at least as bad in public life as they could be in private. The greatness of the scale on which they act, and of the material interests they control, will do little to inspire them. New York and Pennsylvania are by far the largest and wealthiest States in the Union. Their legislatures are confessedly the worst.'131

The passage is the more impressive just because it is not written with a view to Ireland. No one doubts that the people of the United States, both in morality and in talent, equal if they do not excel the people of any other country in the world. But the warmest eulogist of America seeks throughout his work for the explanation of the fact which is really past dispute, that the political morality of the United States sinks below the general morality of the nation.132 There is not the least reason why under a vicious constitution the government at Dublin should not reflect or exaggerate the vices, rather than represent the noble qualities and the gifts, of the Irish people.

But the doctrine of trust takes another and more general form. You may place confidence, it is alleged, in the goodness of human nature, and should believe that the concession of Home Rule, just because it meets the wishes of the Irish people, will take away every source of discontent, and thereby remove any difficulty in making even an imperfect constitution work well.

To this the answer may fairly be made, which I have made in the preceding pages, that Home Rule does not meet the wish of the most important part of the Irish people, but in truth arouses their abhorrence, and that even Home Rulers care much less than Gladstonians suppose about constitutional changes. To give a man a vote for a Parliament at Dublin when he is demanding an acre or two of land, comes very near giving him a stone when he asks for bread. But I assume for a moment that the Irishmen, who express no great enthusiasm for the Home Rule Bill, desire the new constitution as ardently as sixty years or so ago our fathers desired parliamentary reform. Yet even on this assumption the belief in Home Rule as a panacea for Irish ills is childish, and belongs to a bygone stage of opinion. We now know that changes in political machinery, however important, do not of themselves produce content. A poverty-stricken peasant in Connaught will not be made happy because a Parliament meets at Dublin. We now further know that the difficulty of satisfying popular aspirations often arises from the fundamental faults of human nature. Trust in the people may often be wiser than distrust, but to suppose that masses of men are wiser, more reasonable, or more virtuous than the individuals of which they consist, is as idle a political delusion as the corresponding ecclesiastical delusion that a church has virtues denied to the believers who make up the church. On this point an anecdote makes my meaning clearer than an argument. On May 15, 1848, the French National Assembly was invaded by an armed mob, who shouted and yelled for three hours and more, and threatened at any moment to slaughter the representatives of France. From June 22-26, 1848, there raged the most terrible of the insurrections which Paris has seen. For the first time in modern history the workmen of the capital rose against the body of the more or less well-to-do citizens. There was not a man in Paris who did not tremble for his property and his life. Householders feared the very servants in their homes. Between these days of ferocity intervened a day of sentiment. On May 21, 1848, the Assembly attended a Feast of Concord. There were carts filled with allegorical figures, there were processions, there were embraces; the whole town, soldiers, national guards, gardes mobiles, armed workmen, a million of men or more, passed in array before the deputies. The feast was a feast of concord, but every deputy had provided himself with pistols or some weapon of defence. This was the occasion when we are told by the reporter of the scene, 'Carnot said to me with a touch of that silliness (*niaiserie*) which is always to be found mixed up with the virtues of honest democrats, "Believe me, my dear colleague, you must always trust the people." I remember I answered him rather rudely, "Ah! why didn't you remind me of that on the day before May 15?"' The anecdote is told by the greatest political thinker whom France has produced since the days of Montesquieu. 'Trust in the people' did not appear the last word of political wisdom to Alexis de Tocqueville.133

The Gladstonian pleas to which answer has been made are, it will be said, arguments not in favour of our new constitution, but in support of Home Rule. The remark is just; it points to a curious weakness in the reasoning of Gladstonians. They adduce many reasons of more or less weight for conceding some kind of Home Rule to Ireland. But few indeed are the reasons put forward, either in the House of Commons or elsewhere, in favour of the actual Home Rule Bill of 1893. As to the merits of this definite measure Ministerialists show a singular reticence. It may be that they wish to save time and hold that the measure commends itself without any recommendation by force of its own inherent merits. But to a critic of the new constitution another explanation suggests itself. Can it be possible that Ministerialists themselves are not certain what are the fixed principles of the new policy? Everything about it is indefinite, vague, uncertain. Who can say with assurance what Gladstonians understand by Imperial supremacy? Is there or is there not any idea of excluding Ulster from the operation of the Bill? Is it or is it not a principle that members from Ireland shall be summoned to Westminster? Are the Irish members, if summoned, to vote on all matters, or on some only? To each of these questions the only answer that can be given is—nobody knows. But in this state of ignorance it is natural and excusable that apologists should confine themselves to general lines of defence. No politician who respects himself would willingly risk a vigorous apology for the special provisions of a particular measure, when, for aught he knows, the provision which he thinks essential turns out to be an unimportant detail, and is liable to sudden variation.

Chapter V—The Path Of Safety

We stand on the brink of a precipice.134 To say that Englishmen are asked to take a leap in the dark is far to understate the peril of the moment. We are asked to leave an arduous but well-known road, and to spring down an unfathomed ravine filled with rocks, on any one of which we may be dashed to pieces.

The very excess of the peril hides its existence from ordinary citizens. Mr. Gladstone, they argue, is a wise man and a good man, his colleagues are partisans, they are not conspirators; it is incredible that they should recommend a measure fraught with ruin to England. But the matter is intelligible enough. Mr. Gladstone's weakness, no less than his strength, has always lain in his temporary but exclusive preoccupation with some one dominant idea. The one notion which possesses his mind—to judge from his public conduct and speeches—is that at any cost Home Rule, that is, an Irish Executive and an Irish Parliament, must be conceded to Ireland. Enthusiasm, pride, ambition, all the motives, good and bad, which can influence a statesman, urge him to achieve this one object. If he succeeds his political career is crowned with victory, if not with final triumph; if he fails his whole course during the last seven years turns out an error. But it has long been manifest that only with the greatest difficulty can English electors be persuaded to accept Home Rule. Hence it has been found essential that the principles of the measure should not be known before the time for passing it into law. Hence the ill-starred avoidance of discussion. Hence the ultimate framing of a scheme which is made to pass, but is not made to work, and which probably enough does not represent the real wishes or convictions of any one statesman. Where is the Minister who will tell us that this particular Government of Ireland Bill is according to his judgment—I will not say in its details, but in each and all of its leading principles—the best constitution which can be framed for determining the relations between England and Ireland? This Minister has not appeared—I doubt whether he exists. The Bill may be a model of artful provision for conciliating the prejudices or soothing the fears of English electors, but it is not a well-digested constitution. It is inferior to the Home Rule Bill of 1886. Another consequence of the circumstances under which the Bill has been framed is that its authors themselves have never had the benefit to be derived from the mature discussion of its principles. Mr. Gladstone himself cannot say what are and what are not the fundamental ideas of his scheme. He obviously held, at any rate when the Bill was introduced, that the presence of the Irish members at Westminster was a detail, whereas it is in reality the fact which governs the character of the new constitution. To imply that such a matter can be treated as subsidiary is, in the eyes of any student of constitutions, as ridiculous as it would seem to Mr. Gladstone for a Chancellor of the Exchequer, on introducing his budget, to assert that, whether he maintained or did not maintain the income tax, was an organic detail which did not fundamentally affect his financial proposals. The Ministry are as much at sea as their chief; nor is this wonderful. There are two things of which English statesmen have had little experience. The one is a revolutionary movement, the other is the construction of a constitution. But the Home Rule Bill is at once the effect and the sign of a revolutionary movement, and the task in which the Gladstonians are engaged is the formation of a new constitution. Blind leaders are leading a blind people, and our blind leaders, some of whom care more for Radical supremacy in England than for Imperial supremacy in Ireland, are like many other men of our time, the slaves of phrases, such as 'trust in the people,' which pass muster for principles. If the blind lead the blind, what wonder if they stumble over a precipice?

The peril in which the country stands is concealed from us by a curious reaction of opinion. Good political institutions, it was at one time held, were the cause of a nation's happiness, and England, it was firmly believed, owed her prosperity wholly to her constitution. A century of revolutions has taught us all that a good form of government cannot of itself save a state from ruin, and many of us have come to think that forms of government are nothing, and that no constitutional changes can impair the strength of England. No delusion however is more patent or more noxious. Never was a country richer in the elements of strength than were the Thirteen Colonies when their independence was acknowledged by England. Yet the Confederation by the vices of its constitution filled the colonies with discord, and made them both weak at home and contemptible abroad, whilst the creation of the United States restored them to peace and opened for them the road to greatness. The predominance for more than fifty years of the Slave Power in the politics of the American Union, the struggle measured by centuries through which at last the Protestant and progressive Cantons of Switzerland asserted their rightful supremacy over the Catholic and unprogressive Cantons of Switzerland, the weakness of Prussia when, not much more than forty 135 years back, she could hardly maintain her rights and her dignity against Austria, the classical instance of Germany, which though possessed of every source of power lay for generations at the mercy of France, mainly on account of vicious political institutions, are proofs, if evidence were wanting, of the capacity of ill-designed constitutions to hamper the action and threaten the prosperity of great nations. A constitution in truth is a national garb. A good constitution will not make a weak country strong, but an unsuitable constitution may reduce a strong country to feebleness. A weakling does not become a strong man by putting on armour, but a giant can derive no advantage from his strength if once he be got by fraud or force into a strait waistcoat.

Strength, it is true, will in the long run assert itself. The artificial supremacy of Ireland, or of a faction supported by Irish votes, will not last for ever; probably it will not last long. If the new constitution prove unbearable by England it will not be borne; it will be overthrown or evaded. Far am I from asserting that the breach or evasion will, when it shall occur, be justifiable. Englishmen's ideas of good faith are strict, but they are narrow. One main reason for dreading the new constitution is that it may try beyond measure the patience and the honesty of England. If, for instance, Ulster should resist the legal authority of the Parliament at Dublin, there may arise one of those terrible periods in which the observation of pledged faith seems inconsistent with the natural dictates of honour and humanity, and weak concession at the present moment will, at such a crisis, be found to have contained among its other perils the danger lest England, when at last she re-asserts her power in Ireland, should not re-establish her justice.

Where then lies the path of safety? The road is difficult, but it is clearly marked; it is at any rate to be found, not by any exercise of subtlety or of extraordinary acuteness, but by obeying the plain dictates of common sense and sound public morality. The characteristics of Unionist policy must be seriousness, simplicity, and reliance upon an appeal to the nation.

Seriousness is essential.

The need of the time is to impress on the mass of the people the intense gravity of the crisis. Far too much was said before the general election about the weaknesses and the inconsistencies of the Gladstonians, and far too little about the causes of their strength and the absolute necessity for arduous efforts to defeat the Separatists at the polling-booths. The error must not be repeated.

The people must be told, as they may be told with absolute truth, that the fate of England is in question, and that nothing but the efforts of every Unionist throughout the land can save the country from destruction. The contest has, without either party being aware of the change, shifted its character since 1886. Then the names of Unionists and Separatists expressed the whole difference between the opponents and supporters of the Home Rule Bill. The Gladstonians for the most part meant the Bill to affect, as far as possible, the condition of Ireland alone. They did not mean to change the constitution of the United Kingdom. It is now plain, as has been shown throughout these pages, that the measure of so-called Home Rule is a new constitution for the whole United Kingdom. In 1886 the Gladstonians *bona fide* intended to close the period of agitation. In 1893 many Gladstonians see in Home Rule for Ireland only the first step towards an extended scheme of federalism. In 1886 no Gladstonian had palliated crime or oppression, no Gladstonian statesman had discovered that boycotting was nothing but exclusive dealing, no Gladstonian Chancellor had made light of conspiracy. All this is changed. Alliance with revolutionists or conspirators has imbued respectable English statesmen with revolutionary doctrines and revolutionary sentiment. The difference between Unionist and Separatist remains, but it is merged in the wider difference between Constitutionalists and Revolutionists. The question at issue is not merely, though this is serious enough, whether the Act of Union shall be repealed or relaxed, but whether the United Kingdom is morally a nation, and whether as a nation it has a right to insist upon the supreme authority belonging to the majority of its citizens. A similar question was some thirty-two years ago put to the people of the United States; it was decided by the arbitrament of battle.

The terrible calamity of an appeal to the test of force Englishmen may avoid, but if it is to be avoided the national rights of the whole people of the United Kingdom must be asserted as strenuously by their votes as the rights of the citizens of the United States were vindicated by their arms. The people of England again must be solemnly warned that errors in policy or acts of injustice may snatch from us the power of determining a political controversy at the ballot-box instead of on the battle-field. It is folly to raise cases on the constitution; it is always of the most doubtful prudence to handle the casuistry of politics. Nothing will tempt me to discuss in these pages what are the ethical limits to the exercise of constitutionally unlimited sovereignty, or at what point legal oppression justifies armed resistance. Two considerations must at this crisis be kept in mind. The one is that, until oppression is actually committed, the maintenance of order is the duty of every citizen, and, like most political duties, is also a matter of the most obvious expediency; the other is that the compulsion of loyal citizens to forgo the direct protection of the government whose sovereignty they admit, and to accept the rule of a government whose moral claim to their allegiance they deny, is a proceeding of the grossest injustice. Let the people of England also be solemnly warned that the Gladstonian policy of 1893 repeats the essential error of the condemned policy of Protestant ascendency. Gladstonians hold that the democracy of England may ally itself with the democracy of Ireland, and may treat lightly the rights and the wishes of a Protestant and Conservative minority. In bygone times the aristocratic and Protestant government of England allied itself with the Protestant and aristocratic government of Ireland, and held light the rights and the wishes of the Catholic majority. Each policy labours under the same defect. The enforced supremacy of a class, be it a minority or a majority, is opposed to the equitable principle of the supremacy of the whole nation. There is no reason to suppose that Catholic ascendency will be found more tolerable than was Protestant ascendency.

The policy of Unionism should be marked by simplicity.

The Unionist leaders have a clear though a difficult duty to perform. Their one immediate function is resistance to a dangerous revolution. Logically and politically, there was a good deal to be said for the deliberate refusal to discuss, or to vote upon, any of the details of the Home Rule Bill. There is always a danger lest the attempt to amend a radically and essentially vicious measure should promote the delusion that it is amendable. And any success in debate would be dearly purchased if it led the electors to suppose that the Government of Ireland Bill, which in fact embodies a policy, so fundamentally perverse that no alteration of details can render it tolerable, is a measure which, though faulty in its execution, is sound in principle. The Unionists leaders, however, whom we can absolutely trust, have decided that abstention from debate would be an error. As far as the matter is to be looked at from a parliamentary point of view their judgment is decisive, and since the policy of combating the Bill point by point has been adopted it should be carried out, as it is being carried out, with the utmost stringency. Minute discussion of the clauses of the Bill is elaborate instruction for the mass of the nation.

To the cry of obstruction no heed whatever need be paid. As long as there is real discussion obstruction becomes, when the matter in debate is the formation of a new constitution for the United Kingdom, an impossibility. The business needs the most careful consideration. Ministers themselves are uncertain as to what are the essential principles of their own scheme. Every detail involves a principle, and in a Bill where clearness is of vital importance, every clause involves an ambiguity. Each part moreover of the new constitution must be considered with regard to the rest, and the expression of different views as to the meaning of the Bill is of itself of utility, when it is of the greatest importance that Englishmen and Irishmen, Conservatives and Radicals, should be agreed as to the meaning of the new Fundamental Law. When, in short, a constitution for the country is being drawn up, no discussion which is rational can be obstructive. If a week or a fortnight of parliamentary time is expended in defining the meaning of the supreme authority of Parliament, or in deciding whether the Irish delegacy is or is not to be retained at Westminster, not a moment too much is devoted to points of such transcendent importance. 'But the debate,' it is urged, 'will at this rate last for months.' Why not? 'No other Bills,' it is added, 'can be passed.' What Bills, I answer, ought to be passed whilst the constitution of

England is undergoing fundamental alteration? 'But the principles of the measure,' it is objected, 'might have been discussed and settled during the last seven years.' So, I reply, they might, if it had pleased the Gladstonians either to produce their Bill or to announce its general principles. Their silence was politic; it won them a majority at the general election, but you cannot from the nature of things combine the advantages both of reticence and of outspokenness. Silence may have been justified as a piece of clever party tactics; it is a very different question whether the concealment of seven years has turned out high statesmanship. Gladstonians, like other men, cannot, as the saying goes, have their cake and eat it. They have had the advantages, they are now paying the inevitable price of reserve. Unionists in any case are bound to turn this invaluable time to account. Discussion of the constitution is the education of the people.

In order, however, that this political training may be effective, our parliamentary teachers must take care that the public are not confused by the prominence necessarily given to details. Minute criticism of the Bill is important, but at the present moment it is important only as enforcing the radical vice of its main principles. No effort must be spared to keep the mind of the nation well fixed upon these principles. The surrender by the British Parliament and the British Government of all effective part in the government of Ireland, the ambiguities of such a term as 'Imperial supremacy' and all that these ambiguities involve, the inadequacy and the futility of the Restrictions, the errors and impolicy of the financial arrangements, above all the injustice to England and the injury to Ireland of retaining, under a system of Home Rule, even a single Irish representative at Westminster, these broad considerations are the things which should be pressed, and pressed home, upon the electors. Minor matters are good topics for parliamentary discussion, but should not receive a confusing and illusory prominence.

The electors again must be made to feel that it is the essential principle of Home Rule, the setting up of an Irish Government and an Irish Parliament, to which Unionists are opposed. The least appearance of concession to Home Rulers, or any action which gives increased currency to the delusion, certainly cherished by some moderate Gladstonians, that Home Rule can be identified with or cut down to extended local self-government,136 will be fatal to the cause of Unionism. The concession to Ireland of a petty, paltry, peddling legislature, which dare hardly call itself a Parliament, and is officially designated say as a national council, combined with some faint imitation of a Cabinet, called say a committee, would disappoint and irritate Home Rulers; it would cheat their hopes, but it would afford them the means of gaining their end. It would not give assurance to Unionists, it would not be a triumph of Unionist policy, it would rather be the destruction of Unionism. The one course of safety is to take care that at the next general election the country has laid before it for determination a clear and unmistakable issue. The question for every elector to answer must be reducible to the form Aye or No; will you, or will you not, repeal the Union and establish an Irish Executive and an Irish Parliament in Dublin? If the question be so raised Unionists have no reason to fear an answer.

The policy of Unionism has always relied on an appeal to the nation.

The one desire of Unionists has always been to fight their opponents on the clear unmistakable issue of Home Rule. The policy of Separatists has been to keep Home Rule in the background whilst making its meaning indefinite, and to mix up all the multifarious issues raised by the Newcastle programme, as well as many others, with the one essential question whether we should or should not repeal or modify the Act of Union.

To their policy of appeal to the people the Unionists will, of course, adhere. The House of Lords will, it may be presumed, as a matter not so much of right as of obvious duty, reject the present Home Rule Bill, so as to refer to the electors of the United Kingdom the question whether we shall, or shall not, have a new constitution. Even if such a reference to the electors should result in a Gladstonian majority, it is still possible that a further dissolution might be necessary. The majority for Home Rule might be much reduced. I doubt whether Mr. Gladstone himself would maintain that with a majority say of ten or twenty, a Minister would be morally justified in attempting a fundamental change in the constitution. As to such speculative matters there is no need to say anything. It is worth while, however, to repeat a statement which cannot be too often insisted upon, that the most important function of the House of Lords at the present day is to take care that no fundamental change in the constitution takes place which has not received the undoubted assent of the nation. The peers are more and more clearly awakening to the knowledge that under the circumstances of modern public life this protection of the rights of the nation, which is in complete conformity with democratic principle, is the supreme duty of the Upper House.

The question, however, to be considered at the moment is whether for the performance of this duty something more may not be required than the compelling of a dissolution. This something more is a direct appeal to the electors in the nature of a Referendum. The question is still a theoretical one; it cannot (unfortunately as it will appear to many persons) be raised during the debates on the Bill in the House of Commons. When the Bill reaches the House of Lords, it will, we may suppose, be rejected, and all that a Unionist can wish for is, first, that before actual rejection its general principles should be subjected to complete discussion, and what is in this case the same thing, exposure, and next that the House of Lords should, if necessary, take steps which can easily be imagined, for providing that the rejection of the Bill shall entail a dissolution. If, however, the dissolution should result in a Gladstonian majority, and should lead to another Home Rule Bill being sent up to their lordships, the question then arises as to the Referendum. My own conviction, which has been before laid before the public, is that the Lords would do well if they appended to any Home Rule Bill which they were prepared to accept a clause which might make its coming into force depend upon its, within a limited time, receiving the approval of the majority of the electors of the United Kingdom. And in the particular case of the Home Rule Bill it is fair, for reasons already stated,137 that the Bill before becoming law should receive the assent of a majority of the electors both of Great Britain and of Ireland. This course, it may be said, is unconstitutional. This word has no terrors for me; it means no more than unusual, and the institution of a Referendum would simply mean the formal acknowledgment of the doctrine which lies at the basis of English democracy—that a law depends at bottom for its enactment on the assent of the nation as represented by the electors. At a time when the true danger is that sections or classes should arrogate to themselves authority which belongs to the State, it is an advantage to bring into prominence the sovereignty of the nation. The present is exactly a crisis at which we may override the practices to save the principles of the constitution. The most forcible objection which can be made is that you ought not for the sake of avoiding a particular evil to introduce an innovation of dubious expediency. The objection itself is valid, but it is in the present instance inapplicable. My conviction is that the introduction of the Referendum, in one shape or another in respect of large constitutional changes, would be a distinct benefit to the country. It affords the one available check on the recklessness of party leaders; for the check is at once effective and in perfect conformity with democratic principle and sentiment. A second objection is that a Referendum renders any law which obtains the approval of the electors more difficult of alteration than an ordinary Act of Parliament. The allegation is true, but it really tells greatly in favour of an ultimate reference to the people of any Home Rule Bill passed in a Parliament. If such a Bill becomes law, it ought to be a law not admitting of easy repeal. No doubt reaction may be justifiable, but reaction is a great evil, and the Referendum puts a check as well on reaction as on hasty innovation. In any case the time has arrived when Unionist statesmen should consider the expediency of announcing that no Home Rule Bill will finally be accepted until it has undergone a reference to and received the approval of the electors. On no better issue could battle be joined with revolutionists than on the question whether the people of the United Kingdom should or should not be allowed to express their will. Unionists have every reason to feel confidence in their cause; their only policy, their one path of safety is to make it, as they can do, absolutely plain that they rely upon justice, and that they appeal from parties to the nation.

We have now before us the essential features of the new constitution framed by Gladstonians for the whole United Kingdom. We know its inherent defects and inconsistencies; we have considered what may be said on its behalf, or rather of the policy of which it is the outcome. The proposed change in our form of government touches the very foundations of the State, and deeply, though indirectly, threatens the unity of the whole Empire. Never surely since the day when the National Assembly of France drew up that Constitution of 1791, which built to be eternal endured for not quite a year, has an ancient nation been so strangely invited to accept an untried and unknown polity.

The position indeed of the French constitution-makers was in some respects stronger and more defensible than the position of our English innovators. The members of the National Assembly knew precisely what they were doing. They meant to alter the fundamental institutions of France. A change moreover in the whole scheme of French government was an admitted necessity. France might be uncertain as to the working of the new constitution, but France was absolutely certain that the *ancien régime* was detestable. Individuals or nations may wisely risk much when they are escaping from a social condition which they detest, they may know that an innovation is in itself of doubtful expediency, yet may consider any alleged reform worth a trial when no change can be a change for the worse. In the France of 1791 confidence in the future meant abhorrence of the past.

The authors of our new constitution can hardly be called the designers of their own handiwork; they have been the sport of accident. Their intention, or rather the intention of their leader, was in 1886 merely to grant some sort of Parliamentary independence to Ireland. The resolution to concede Home Rule was sudden; it may have been taken up without due weighing of its consequences. It has assuredly led to unexpected results. The statesmen who meant merely to give Home Rule to Ireland have stumbled into the making of a new constitution for the United Kingdom. What wonder that their workmanship betrays its accidental origin. It has no coherence, no consistency; nothing is called by its right name, and words are throughout substituted for facts; the new Parliament of Ireland is denied its proper title; the supremacy of the Imperial Parliament is nominally saved, and is really destroyed; and the very statesmen who proclaim the supremacy of the Imperial Parliament refuse to assert the subordination of the Irish Parliament. The authors of the constitution are at sea as to its leading principles, and its most essential provision they deem an organic detail, which may at any moment be modified or removed. The whole thing is an incongruous patchwork affair, made up of shreds and tatters torn from the institutions of other lands. It is as inconsistent with the proposed and rejected Constitution of 1886 as with the existing Constitution of England. While however our constitution-makers tender for the acceptance of the nation a scheme of fundamental change, whereof the effect is uncertain, conjectural, and perilous, and the permanence is not guaranteed by its authors, Englishmen are well satisfied with their old constitution; they may desire its partial modification or expansion, they have never even contemplated its overthrow. Politicians, in short, who meant to initiate a moderate reform, are pressing a revolutionary change on a country which neither needs nor desires a revolution; they propose to get rid of grave, though temporary, inconveniences by a permanent alteration of which no man can calculate the results in our whole system of government. Never before was a nation so strangely advised by such bewildered counsellors to take for so little apparent reason so desperate a leap in the dark.

Appendix

Government Of Ireland Bill

ARRANGEMENT OF CLAUSES

Legislative Authority

Clause.

1. Establishment of Irish Legislature.

2. Powers of Irish Legislature.

3. Exceptions from powers of Irish Legislature.

4. Restrictions on powers of Irish Legislature.

Executive Authority

5. Executive power in Ireland.

Constitution of Legislature

6. Composition of Irish Legislative Council.

7. Composition of Irish Legislative Assembly.

8. Disagreement between two Houses, how settled.

Irish Representation in House of Commons

9. Representation in Parliament of Irish counties and boroughs.

Finance

10. As to separate Consolidated Fund and taxes.

11. Hereditary revenues and income tax.

12. Financial arrangements as between United Kingdom and Ireland.

13. Treasury Account (Ireland).

14. Charges on Irish Consolidated Fund.

15. Irish Church Fund.

16. Local loans.

17. Adaptation of Acts as to Local Taxation Accounts and probate, etc., duties.

18. Money bills and votes.

19. Exchequer judges for revenue actions, election petitions, etc.

Post Office Postal Telegraphs and Savings Banks

20. Transfer of post office and postal telegraphs.

21. Transfer of savings banks.

Irish Appeals and Decision of Constitutional Questions

22. Irish appeals.

23. Special provision for decision of constitutional questions.

Lord Lieutenant and Crown Lands

24. Office of Lord Lieutenant.

25. Use of Crown lands by Irish Government.

Judges and Civil Servants

26. Tenure of future judges.

27. As to existing judges and other persons having salaries charged on the Consolidated Fund.

28. As to persons holding civil service appointments.

29. As to existing pensions and superannuation allowances.

Police

30. As to Police.

Miscellaneous

31. Irish Exchequer Consolidated Fund and Audit.

32. Law applicable to both Houses of Irish Legislature.

33. Supplemental provisions as to powers of Irish Legislature.

34. Limitation on borrowing by local authorities.

Transitory Provisions

35. Temporary restriction on powers of Irish Legislature and Executive.

36. Transitory provisions.

37. Continuance of existing laws, courts, officers, etc.

38. Appointed day.

39. Definitions.

40. Short title.

SCHEDULES

A Bill To Amend The Provision For The Government Of Ireland138

Whereas it is expedient that without impairing or restricting the supreme authority of Parliament, an Irish Legislature should be created for such purposes in Ireland as in this Act mentioned:

Be it therefore enacted by the Queen's most Excellent Majesty, by and with the advice and consent of the Lords Spiritual and Temporal, and Commons, in this present Parliament assembled, and by the authority of the same, as follows:

Legislative Authority

1. *On and after the appointed day* there shall be in Ireland a Legislature consisting of Her Majesty the Queen and of two Houses, the Legislative Council and the Legislative Assembly.

2. With the exceptions and subject to the restrictions in this Act mentioned, there shall be granted to the Irish Legislature power to make laws for the peace, order, and good government of Ireland in respect of matters exclusively relating to Ireland or some part thereof.

3. The Irish Legislature shall not have power to make laws in respect of the following matters or any of them:—

(1) The Crown, or the succession to the Crown, or a Regency; or the Lord Lieutenant as representative of the Crown; or

(2) The making of peace or war or matters arising from a state of war; or

(3) Naval or military forces, or the defence of the realm; or

(4) Treaties and other relations with foreign States or the relations between different parts of Her Majesty's dominions or offences connected with such treaties or relations; or

(5) Dignities or titles of honour; or

(6) Treason, treason-felony, alienage, or naturalisation; or

(7) Trade with any place out of Ireland; or quarantine, or navigation (except as respects inland waters and local health or harbour regulations); or

(8) Beacons, lighthouses, or sea marks (except so far as they can consistently

with any general Act of Parliament be constructed or maintained by a local harbour authority); or

(9) Coinage; legal tender; or the standard of weights and measures; or

(10) Trade marks, merchandise marks, copyright, or patent rights.

Any law made in contravention of this section shall be void.

4. The powers of the Irish Legislature shall not extend to the making of any law—

(1) Respecting the establishment or endowment of religion, or prohibiting the free exercise thereof; or

(2) Imposing any disability, or conferring any privilege, on account of religious belief; or

(3) Abrogating or prejudicially affecting the right to establish or maintain any place of denominational education or any denominational institution or charity; or

(4) Prejudicially affecting the right of any child to attend a school receiving public money, without attending the religious instruction at that school; or

(5) Whereby any person may be deprived of life, liberty, or property without due process of law, or may be denied the equal protection of the laws, or whereby private property may be taken without just compensation; or

(6) Whereby any existing corporation incorporated by Royal Charter or by any local or general Act of Parliament (not being a corporation raising for public purposes taxes, rates, cess, dues, or tolls, or administering funds so raised) may, unless it consents, or the leave of Her Majesty is first obtained on address from the two Houses of the Irish Legislature, be deprived of its rights, privileges, or property without due process of law; or

(7) Whereby any inhabitant of the United Kingdom may be deprived of equal rights as respects public sea fisheries.

Any law made in contravention of this section shall be void.

Executive Authority

5.—(1) The executive power in Ireland shall continue vested in Her Majesty the Queen, and the Lord Lieutenant, on behalf of Her Majesty, shall exercise any prerogatives or other executive power of the Queen the exercise of which may be delegated to him by Her Majesty, and shall, in Her Majesty's name, summon, prorogue, and dissolve the Irish Legislature.

(2) There shall be an Executive Committee of the Privy Council of Ireland to

aid and advise in the government of Ireland, being of such numbers, and comprising persons holding such offices, as Her Majesty may think fit, or as may be directed by Irish Act.

(3) The Lord Lieutenant shall, on the advice of the said Executive Committee, give or withhold the assent of Her Majesty to Bills passed by the two Houses of the Irish Legislature, subject nevertheless to any instructions given by Her Majesty in respect of any such Bill.

Constitution of Legislature

6.—(1) The Irish Legislative Council shall consist of *forty-eight* councillors.

(2) Each of the constituencies mentioned in the First Schedule to this Act shall return the number of councillors named opposite thereto in the schedule.

(3) Every man shall be entitled to be registered as an elector, and when registered to vote at an election, of a councillor for a constituency, who owns or occupies any land or tenement in the constituency of a rateable value of more than *twenty* pounds, subject to the like conditions as a man is entitled at the passing of this Act to be registered and vote as a parliamentary elector in respect of an ownership qualification or of the qualification specified in section five of the Representation of the People Act, 1884, as the case may be: Provided that a man shall not be entitled to be registered, nor if registered to vote, at an election of a councillor in more than one constituency in the same year.

(4) The term of office of every councillor shall be *eight* years, and shall not be affected by a dissolution; and one *half* of the councillors shall retire in every *fourth* year, and their seats shall be filled by a new election.

7.—(1) The Irish Legislative Assembly shall consist of *one hundred and three* members, returned by the existing parliamentary constituencies in Ireland, or the existing divisions thereof, and elected by the parliamentary electors for the time being in those constituencies or divisions.

(2) The Irish Legislative Assembly when summoned may, unless sooner dissolved, have continuance *for five* years from the day on which the summons directs it to meet and no longer.

(3) After *six* years from the passing of this Act, the Irish Legislature may alter the qualification of the electors, and the constituencies, and the distribution of the members among the constituencies, provided that in such distribution due regard is had to the population of the constituencies.

8. If a Bill or any provision of a Bill adopted by the Legislative Assembly is lost by the disagreement of the Legislative Council, and after a dissolution, or

the period of *two years* from such disagreement, such Bill, or a Bill for enacting the said provision, is again adopted by the Legislative Assembly and fails within three months afterwards to be adopted by the Legislative Council, the same shall forthwith be submitted to the members of the two Houses deliberating and voting together thereon, and shall be adopted or rejected according to the decision of the majority of those members present and voting on the question.

Irish Representation in House of Commons

9. Unless and until Parliament otherwise determines, the following provisions shall have effect—

(1) After *the appointed day* each of the constituencies named in the Second Schedule to this Act shall return to serve in Parliament the number of members named opposite thereto in that schedule, and no more, and Dublin University shall cease to return any member.

(2) The existing divisions of the constituencies shall, save as provided in that schedule, be abolished.

(3) An Irish representative peer in the House of Lords and a member of the House of Commons for an Irish constituency shall not be entitled to deliberate or vote on—

(a) any Bill or motion in relation thereto, the operation of which Bill or motion is confined to Great Britain or some part thereof; or

(b) any motion or resolution relating solely to some tax not raised or to be raised in Ireland; or

(c) any vote or appropriation of money made exclusively for some service not mentioned in the Third Schedule to this Act; or

(d) any motion or resolution exclusively affecting Great Britain or some part thereof or some local authority or some person or thing therein; or

(e) any motion or resolution, incidental to any such motion or resolution as either is last mentioned, or relates solely to some tax not raised or to be raised in Ireland, or incidental to any such vote or appropriation of money as aforesaid.

(4) Compliance with the provisions of this section shall not be questioned otherwise than in each House in manner provided by the House.

(5) The election laws and the laws relating to the qualification of parliamentary electors shall not, so far as they relate to parliamentary elections, be altered by the Irish Legislature, but this enactment shall not prevent the Irish Legislature from dealing with any officers concerned with

the issue of writs of election, and if any officers are so dealt with, it shall be lawful for Her Majesty by Order in Council to arrange for the issue of such writs, and the writs issued in pursuance of such Order shall be of the same effect as if issued in manner heretofore accustomed.

Finance

10.—(1) *On and after the appointed day* there shall be an Irish Exchequer and Consolidated Fund separate from those of the United Kingdom.

(2) The duties of customs and excise and the duties on postage shall be imposed by Act of Parliament, but subject to the provisions of this Act the Irish Legislature may, in order to provide for the public service of Ireland, impose any other taxes.

(3) Save as in this Act mentioned, all matters relating to the taxes in Ireland and the collection and management thereof shall be regulated by Irish Act, and the same shall be collected and managed by the Irish Government and form part of the public revenues of Ireland: Provided that—

(a) the duties of customs shall be regulated, collected, managed, and paid into the Exchequer of the United Kingdom as heretofore; and

(b) all prohibitions in connection with the duties of excise, and so far as regards articles sent out of Ireland, all matters relating to those duties, shall be regulated by Act of Parliament; and

(c) the excise duties on articles consumed in Great Britain shall be paid in Great Britain or to an officer of the Government of the United Kingdom.

(4) Save as in this Act mentioned, all the public revenues of Ireland shall be paid into the Irish Exchequer and form a Consolidated Fund, and be appropriated to the public service of Ireland by Irish Act.

(5) If the duties of excise are increased above the rates in force on *the first day of March one thousand eight hundred and ninety-three*, the net proceeds in Ireland of the duties in excess of the said rates shall be paid from the Irish Exchequer to the Exchequer of the United Kingdom.

(6) *If the duties of excise are reduced below the rates in force on the said day, and the net proceeds of such duties in Ireland are in consequence less than the net proceeds of the duties before the reduction, a sum equal to the deficiency shall, unless it is otherwise agreed between the Treasury and the Irish Government, be paid from the Exchequer of the United Kingdom to the Irish Exchequer.*

11. —(1) The hereditary revenues of the Crown in Ireland which are managed by the Commissioners of Woods shall continue during the life of Her present

Majesty to be managed and collected by those Commissioners, and the net amount payable by them to the Exchequer on account of those revenues, after deducting all expenses (but including an allowance for interest on such proceeds of the sale of those revenues as have not been re-invested in Ireland), shall be paid into the Treasury Account (Ireland) hereinafter mentioned, for the benefit of the Irish Exchequer.

(2) A person shall not be required to pay income tax in Great Britain in respect of property situate or business carried on in Ireland, and a person shall not be required to pay income tax in Ireland in respect of property situate or business carried on in Great Britain.

(3) *For the purpose of giving to Ireland the benefit of the difference between the income tax collected in Great Britain from British, Colonial, and foreign securities held by residents in Ireland, and the income tax collected in Ireland from Irish securities held by residents in Great Britain, there shall be made to Ireland out of the income tax collected in Great Britain, an allowance of such amount as may be from time to time determined by the Treasury, in accordance with a minute of the Treasury laid before Parliament before the appointed day, and such allowance shall be paid into the Treasury Account (Ireland) for the benefit of the Irish Exchequer.*

(4) Provided that the provisions of this section with respect to income tax shall not apply to any excess of the rate of income tax in Great Britain above the rate in Ireland or of the rate of income tax in Ireland above the rate in Great Britain.

12.—(1) The duties of customs contributed by Ireland and, save as provided by this Act, that portion of any public revenue of the United Kingdom to which Ireland may claim to be entitled, whether specified in the Third Schedule to this Act or not, shall be carried to the Consolidated Fund of the United Kingdom, as the contribution of Ireland to Imperial liabilities and expenditure as defined in that Schedule.

(2) The civil charges of the Government in Ireland shall, subject as in this Act mentioned, be borne after the appointed day by Ireland.

(3) After *fifteen* years from the passing of this Act the arrangements made by this Act for the contribution of Ireland to Imperial liabilities and expenditure, and otherwise for the financial relations between the United Kingdom and Ireland, may be revised in pursuance of an address to Her Majesty from the House of Commons, or from the Irish Legislative Assembly.

13.—(1) There shall be established under the direction of the Treasury an account (in this Act referred to as the Treasury Account (Ireland)).

(2) There shall be paid into such account all sums payable from the Irish Exchequer to the Exchequer of the United Kingdom, or from the latter to the former Exchequer, and all sums directed to be paid into the account for the benefit of either of the said Exchequers.

(3) All sums which are payable from either of the said Exchequers to the other of them, or being payable out of one of the said Exchequers are repayable by the other Exchequer, shall in the first instance be payable out of the said account so far as the money standing on the account is sufficient; and for the purpose of meeting such sums, the Treasury out of the customs revenue collected in Ireland, and the Irish Government out of any of the public revenues in Ireland, may direct money to be paid to the Treasury Account (Ireland) instead of into the Exchequer.

(4) Any surplus standing on the account to the credit of either Exchequer, and not required for meeting payments, shall at convenient times be paid into that Exchequer, and where any sum so payable into the Exchequer of the United Kingdom is required by law to be forthwith paid to the National Debt Commissioners, that sum may be paid to those Commissioners without being paid into the Exchequer.

(5) All sums payable by virtue of this Act out of the Consolidated Fund of the United Kingdom or of Ireland shall be payable from the Exchequer of the United Kingdom or Ireland, as the case may be, within the meaning of this Act, and all sums by this Act made payable from the Exchequer of the United Kingdom shall, if not otherwise paid, be charged on and paid out of the Consolidated Fund of the United Kingdom.

14.—(1) There shall be charged on the Irish Consolidated Fund in favour of the Exchequer of the United Kingdom as a first charge on that fund all sums which—

(a) are payable to that Exchequer from the Irish Exchequer; or

(b) are required to repay to the Exchequer of the United Kingdom sums issued to meet the dividends or sinking fund on guaranteed land stock under the Purchase of Land (Ireland) Act, 1891, or

(c) otherwise have been or are required to be paid out of the Exchequer of the United Kingdom in consequence of the non-payment thereof out of the Exchequer of Ireland or otherwise by the Irish Government.

(2) If at any time the Controller and Auditor-General of the United Kingdom is satisfied that any such charge is due, he shall certify the amount of it, and the Treasury shall send such certificate to the Lord Lieutenant, who shall thereupon by order, without any counter-signature, direct the payment of the

amount from the Irish Exchequer to the Exchequer of the United Kingdom, and such order shall be duly obeyed by all persons, and until the amount is wholly paid no other payment shall be made out of the Irish Exchequer for any purpose whatever.

(3) There shall be charged on the Irish Consolidated Fund next after the foregoing charge:

(a) all sums, for dividends or sinking fund on guaranteed land stock under the Purchase of Land (Ireland) Act, 1891, which the Land Purchase Account and the Guarantee Fund under that Act are insufficient to pay;

(b) all sums due in respect of any debt incurred by the Government of Ireland, whether for interest, management, or sinking fund;

(c) an annual sum of *five thousand* pounds for the expenses of the household and establishment of the Lord Lieutenant;

(d) all existing charges on the Consolidated Fund of the United Kingdom in respect of Irish services other than the salary of the Lord Lieutenant; and

(e) the salaries and pensions of all judges of the Supreme Court or other superior court in Ireland or of any county or other like court, who are appointed after the passing of this Act, and are not the Exchequer judges hereafter mentioned.

(4) Until all charges created by this Act upon the Irish Consolidated Fund and for the time being due are paid, no money shall be issued from the Irish Exchequer for any other purpose whatever.

15.—(1) All existing charges on the Church property in Ireland—that is to say, all property accruing under the Irish Church Act, 1869, and transferred to the Irish Land Commission by the Irish Church Amendment Act, 1881—shall so far as not paid out of the said property be charged on the Irish Consolidated Fund, and any of those charges guaranteed by the Treasury, if and so far as not paid, shall be paid out of the Exchequer of the United Kingdom.

(2) Subject to the existing charges thereon, the said Church property shall belong to the Irish Government, and be managed, administered, and disposed of as directed by Irish Act.

16.—(1) All sums paid or applicable in or towards the discharge of the interest or principal of any local loan advanced before the appointed day on security in Ireland, or otherwise in respect of such loan, which but for this Act would be paid to the National Debt Commissioners, and carried to the Local Loans Fund, shall, after the appointed day, be paid, until otherwise provided by Irish Act, to the Irish Exchequer.

(2) For the payment to the Local Loans Fund of the principal and interest of such loans, the Irish Government shall after the appointed day pay by half-yearly payments an annuity for *forty-nine* years, at the rate of *four* per cent, on the principal of the said loans, exclusive of any sums written off before the appointed day from the account of assets of the Local Loans Fund, and such annuity shall be paid from the Irish Exchequer to the Exchequer of the United Kingdom, and when so paid shall be forthwith paid to the National Debt Commissioners for the credit of the Local Loans Fund.

(3) After the appointed day, money for loans in Ireland shall cease to be advanced either by the Public Works Loan Commissioners or out of the Local Loans Fund.

17.—(1) So much of any Act as directs payment to the Local Taxation (Ireland) Account of any share of probate, excise, or customs duties payable to the Exchequer of the United Kingdom shall, together with any enactment amending the same, be repealed as from the appointed day without prejudice to the adjustment of balances after that day; but the like amounts shall continue to be paid to the Local Taxation Accounts in England and Scotland as would have been paid if this Act had not passed, and any residue of the said share shall be paid into the Exchequer of the United Kingdom.

(2) The stamp duty chargeable in respect of the personalty of a deceased person shall not in the case of administration granted in Great Britain be chargeable in respect of any personalty situate in Ireland, nor in the case of administration granted in Ireland be chargeable in respect of any personalty situate in Great Britain; and any administration granted in Great Britain shall not, if re-sealed in Ireland, be exempt from stamp duty on administration granted in Ireland, and any administration granted in Ireland shall not, when re-sealed in Great Britain, be exempt from stamp duty on administration granted in Great Britain.

(3) In this section the expression "administration" means probate or letters of administration, and as respects Scotland, confirmation inclusive of the inventory required under the Acts relating to the said stamp duty, and the expression "personalty" means personal or movable estate and effects.

18.—(1) Bills for appropriating any part of the public revenue or for imposing any tax shall originate in the Legislative Assembly.

(2) It shall not be lawful for the Legislative Assembly to adopt or pass any vote, resolution, address, or Bill for the appropriation for any purpose of any part of the public revenue of Ireland, or of any tax, except in pursuance of a recommendation from the Lord Lieutenant in the session in which such vote, resolution, address, or Bill is proposed.

19.—(1) Two of the judges of the Supreme Court in Ireland shall be Exchequer judges, and shall be appointed under the great seal of the United Kingdom; and their salaries and pensions shall be charged on and paid out of the Consolidated Fund of the United Kingdom.

(2) The Exchequer judges shall be removeable only by Her Majesty on address from the two Houses of Parliament, and each such judge shall, save as otherwise provided by Parliament, receive the same salary and be entitled to the same pension as is at the time of his appointment fixed for the puisne judges of the Supreme Court, and during his continuance in office his salary shall not be diminished, nor his right to pension altered, without his consent.

(3) An alteration of any rules relating to such legal proceedings as are mentioned in this section shall not be made except with the approval of Her Majesty the Queen in Council; and the sittings of the Exchequer judges shall be regulated with the like approval.

(4) All legal proceedings in Ireland, which are instituted at the instance of or against the Treasury or Commissioners of Customs, or any of their officers, or relate to the election of members to serve in Parliament, or touch any matter within the powers of the Irish Legislature, or touch any matter affected by a law which the Irish Legislature have not power to repeal or alter, shall, if so required by any party to such proceedings, be heard and determined before the Exchequer judges or (except where the case requires to be determined by two judges) before one of them, and in any such legal proceeding an appeal shall, if any party so requires, lie from any court of first instance in Ireland to the Exchequer judges, and the decision of the Exchequer judges shall be subject to appeal to Her Majesty the Queen in Council and not to any other tribunal.

(5) If it is made to appear to an Exchequer judge that any decree or judgment in any such proceeding as aforesaid has not been duly enforced by the sheriff or other officer whose duty it is to enforce the same, such judge shall appoint some officer whose duty it shall be to enforce the judgment or decree; and for that purpose such officer and all persons employed by him shall be entitled to the same privileges, immunities, and powers as are by law conferred on a sheriff and his officers.

(6) The Exchequer judges, when not engaged in hearing and determining such legal proceedings as above in this section mentioned, shall perform such of the duties ordinarily performed by other judges of the Supreme Court in Ireland as may be assigned by Her Majesty the Queen in Council.

(7) All sums recovered by the Treasury or the Commissioners of Customs or any of their officers, or recovered under any Act relating to duties of customs,

shall, notwithstanding anything in any other Act, be paid to such public account as the Treasury or the Commissioners direct.

Post Office Postal Telegraphs and Savings Banks

20.—(1) As from *the appointed day* the postal and telegraph service in Ireland shall be transferred to the Irish Government, and may be regulated by Irish Act, except as in this Act mentioned and except as regards matters relating—

(a) to such conditions of the transmission or delivery of postal packets and telegrams as are incidental to the duties on postage; or

(b) foreign mails or submarine telegraphs or through lines in connection therewith; or

(c) to any other postal or telegraph business in connection with places out of the United Kingdom.

(2) The administration of or incidental to the said excepted matters shall, save as may be otherwise arranged with the Irish Post Office, remain with the Postmaster-General.

(3) As regards the revenue and expenses of the postal and telegraph service, the Postmaster-General shall retain the revenue collected and defray the expenses incurred in Great Britain, and the Irish Post Office shall retain the revenue collected and defray the expenses incurred in Ireland, subject to the provisions of the Fourth Schedule to this Act; which schedule shall have full effect, but may be varied or added to by agreement between the Postmaster-General and the Irish Post Office.

(4) *The sums payable by the Postmaster-General or Irish Post Office to the other of them in pursuance of this Act shall, if not paid out of the Post Office moneys, be paid from the Exchequer of the United Kingdom or of Ireland, as the case requires, to the other Exchequer.*

(5) Sections forty-eight to fifty-two of the Telegraph Act 1863, and any enactment amending the same, shall apply to all telegraphic lines of the Irish Government in like manner as to the telegraphs of a company within the meaning of that Act.

21.—(1) As from *the appointed day* there shall be transferred to the Irish Government the post office savings banks in Ireland and all such powers and duties of any department or officer in Great Britain as are connected with post office savings banks, trustee savings banks or friendly societies in Ireland, and the same may be regulated by Irish Act.

(2) The Treasury shall publish not less than six months' previous notice of the transfer of savings banks.

(3) If before the date of the transfer any depositor in a post office savings bank so requests, his deposit shall, according to his request, either be paid to him or transferred to a post office savings bank in Great Britain, and after the said date the depositors in a post office savings bank in Ireland shall cease to have any claim against the Postmaster-General or the Consolidated Fund of the United Kingdom, but shall have the like claim against the Government and Consolidated Fund of Ireland.

(4) If before the date of the transfer the trustees of any trustee savings bank so request, then, according to the request, either all sums due to them shall be repaid and the savings bank closed, or those sums shall be paid to the Irish Government, and after the said date the trustees shall cease to have any claim against the National Debt Commissioners or the Consolidated Fund of the United Kingdom, but shall have the like claim against the Government and Consolidated Fund of Ireland.

(5) Notwithstanding the foregoing provisions of this section, if a sum due on account of any annuity or policy of insurance which has before the above-mentioned notice been granted through a post office or trustee savings bank is not paid by the Irish Government, that sum shall be paid out of the Exchequer of the United Kingdom.

Irish Appeals and Decision of Constitutional Questions

22.—(1) The appeal from courts in Ireland to the House of Lords shall cease; and where any person would, but for this Act, have a right to appeal from any court in Ireland to the House of Lords, such person shall have the like right to appeal to Her Majesty the Queen in Council; and the right so to appeal shall not be affected by any Irish Act; and all enactments relating to appeals to Her Majesty the Queen in Council, and to the Judicial Committee of the Privy Council, shall apply accordingly.

(2) When the Judicial Committee sit for hearing appeals from a court in Ireland, there shall be present not less than four Lords of Appeal, within the meaning of the Appellate Jurisdiction Act, 1876, and at least one member who is or has been a judge of the Supreme Court in Ireland.

(3) A rota of privy councillors to sit for hearing appeals from courts in Ireland shall be made annually by Her Majesty in Council, and the privy councillors, or some of them, on that rota shall sit to hear the said appeals. A casual vacancy in such rota during the year may be filled by Order in Council.

(4) Nothing in this Act shall affect the jurisdiction of the House of Lords to determine the claims to Irish peerages.

23.—(1) If it appears to the Lord Lieutenant or a Secretary of State expedient in the public interest that steps shall be taken for the speedy determination of the question whether any Irish Act or any provision thereof is beyond the powers of the Irish Legislature, he may represent the same to Her Majesty in Council, and thereupon the said question shall be forthwith referred to and heard and determined by the Judicial Committee of the Privy Council, constituted as if hearing an appeal from a court in Ireland.

(2) Upon the hearing of the question such persons as seem to the Judicial Committee to be interested may be allowed to appear and be heard as parties to the case, and the decision of the Judicial Committee shall be given in like manner as if it were the decision of an appeal, the nature of the report or recommendation to Her Majesty being stated in open court.

(3) Nothing in this Act shall prejudice any other power of Her Majesty in Council to refer any question to the Judicial Committee or the right of any person to petition Her Majesty for such reference.

Lord Lieutenant and Crown Lands

24.—(1) Notwithstanding anything to the contrary in any Act, every subject of the Queen shall be qualified to hold the office of Lord Lieutenant of Ireland, without reference to his religious belief.

(2) The term of office of the Lord Lieutenant shall be *six years*, without prejudice to the power of Her Majesty the Queen at any time to revoke the appointment. 25. Her Majesty the Queen in Council may place under the control of the Irish Government, for the purposes of that government, such of the lands and buildings in Ireland vested in or held in trust for Her Majesty, and subject to such conditions or restrictions (if any) as may seem expedient.

Judges and Civil Servants

26. A judge of the Supreme Court or other superior court in Ireland, or of any county court or other court with a like jurisdiction in Ireland, appointed after the passing of this Act, shall not be removed from his office except in pursuance of an address from the two Houses of the Legislature of Ireland, nor during his continuance in office shall his salary be diminished or right to pension altered without his consent.

27.—(1) All existing judges of the Supreme Court, county court judges, and Land Commissioners in Ireland and all existing officers serving in Ireland in the permanent civil service of the Crown and receiving salaries charged on the Consolidated Fund of the United Kingdom, shall, if they are removeable at present on address from both Houses of Parliament, continue to be removeable only upon such address, and if removeable in any other manner shall continue to be removeable only in the same manner as heretofore; and shall continue to receive the same salaries, gratuities, and pensions, and to be liable to perform the same duties as heretofore, or such duties as Her Majesty may declare to be analogous, and their salaries and pensions, if and so far as not paid out of the Irish Consolidated Fund, shall be paid out of the Exchequer of the United Kingdom: Provided that this section shall be subject to the provisions of this Act with respect to the Exchequer judges.

(2) If any of the said judges, commissioners, or officers retires from office with the Queen's approbation before completion of the period of service entitling him to a pension, Her Majesty may, if she thinks fit, grant to him such pension, not exceeding the pension to which he would on that completion have been entitled, as to Her Majesty seems meet.

28.—(1) All existing officers in the permanent civil service of the Crown, who are not above provided for, and are at the appointed day serving in Ireland, shall after that day continue to hold their offices by the same tenure and to receive the same salaries, gratuities, and pensions, and to be liable to perform the same duties as heretofore or such duties as the Treasury may declare to be analogous; *and the said gratuities and pensions, and until three years after the passing of this Act, the salaries due to any of the said officers if remaining in his existing office, shall be paid to the payees by the Treasury out of the Exchequer of the United Kingdom.*

(2) Any such officer may after *three years* from the passing of this Act retire from office, and shall, at any time during those three years, if required by the Irish Government, retire from office, and on any such retirement may be awarded by the Treasury a gratuity or pension in accordance with the Fifth Schedule to this Act; Provided that—

(a) six months' written notice shall, unless it is otherwise agreed, be given either by the said officer or by the Irish Government as the case requires; and

(b) such number of officers only shall retire at one time and at such intervals of time as the Treasury, in communication with the Irish Government, sanction.

(3) If any such officer does not so retire, the Treasury may award him after the said three years a pension in accordance with the Fifth Schedule to this Act which shall become payable to him on his ultimate retirement from the service of the Crown.

(4) The gratuities and pensions awarded in accordance with the Fifth Schedule to this Act shall be paid by the Treasury to the payees out of the Exchequer of the United Kingdom.

(5) All sums paid out of the Exchequer of the United Kingdom in pursuance

of this section shall be repaid to that Exchequer from the Irish Exchequer.

(6) This section shall not apply to officers retained in the service of the Government of the United Kingdom.

29. Any existing pension granted on account of service in Ireland as a judge of the Supreme Court or of any court consolidated into that court, or as a county court judge, or in any other judicial position, or as an officer in the permanent civil service of the Crown other than in an office the holder of which is after the appointed day retained in the service of the Government of the United Kingdom, shall be charged on the Irish Consolidated Fund, and if and so far as not paid out of that fund, shall be paid out of the Exchequer of the United Kingdom.

Police

30.—(1) The forces of the Royal Irish Constabulary and Dublin Metropolitan Police shall, when and as local police forces are from time to time established in Ireland in accordance with the Sixth Schedule to this Act, be gradually reduced and ultimately cease to exist as mentioned in that Schedule; and after the passing of this Act, no officer or man shall be appointed to either of those forces;

Provided that until the expiration of *six* years from the appointed day, nothing in this Act shall require the Lord Lieutenant to cause either of the said forces to cease to exist, if as representing Her Majesty the Queen he considers it inexpedient.

(2) The said two forces shall, while they continue, be subject to the control of the Lord Lieutenant as representing Her Majesty, and the members thereof shall continue to receive the same salaries, gratuities, and pensions, and hold their appointments on the same tenure as heretofore, *and those salaries, gratuities, and pensions, and all the expenditure incidental to either force, shall be paid out of the Exchequer of the United Kingdom.*

(3) When any existing member of either force retires under the provisions of the Sixth Schedule to this Act, the Treasury may award to him a gratuity or pension in accordance with that Schedule.

(4) *Those gratuities and pensions and all existing pensions payable in respect of service in either force, shall be paid by the Treasury to the payees out of the Exchequer of the United Kingdom.*

(5) *Two-thirds of the net amount payable in pursuance of this section out of the Exchequer of the United Kingdom shall be repaid to that Exchequer from the Irish Exchequer.*

Miscellaneous

31. Save as may be otherwise provided by Irish Act—

(a) The existing law relating to the Exchequer and Consolidated Fund of the United Kingdom shall apply with the necessary modifications to the Exchequer and Consolidated Fund of Ireland, and an officer shall be appointed by the Lord Lieutenant to be the Irish Comptroller and Auditor General; and

(b) The accounts of the Irish Consolidated Fund shall be audited as appropriation accounts in manner provided by the Exchequer and Audit Departments Act, 1866, by or under the direction of such officer.

32.—(1) Subject as in this Act mentioned and particularly to the Seventh Schedule to this Act (which Schedule shall have full effect) all existing election laws relating to the House of Commons and the members thereof shall, so far as applicable, extend to each of the two Houses of the Irish Legislature and the members thereof, but such election laws so far as hereby extended may be altered by Irish Act.

(2) The privileges, rights, and immunities to be held and enjoyed by each House and the members thereof shall be such as may be defined by Irish Act, but so that the same shall never exceed those for the time being held and enjoyed by the House of Commons, and the members thereof.

33.—(i) The Irish Legislature may repeal or alter any provision of this Act which is by this Act expressly made alterable by that Legislature, and also any enactments in force in Ireland, except such as either relate to matters beyond the powers of the Irish Legislature, or being enacted by Parliament after the passing of this Act may be expressly extended to Ireland. An Irish Act, notwithstanding it is in any respect repugnant to any enactment excepted as aforesaid, shall, though read subject to that enactment, be, except to the extent of that repugnancy, valid.

(2) An order, rule, or regulation, made in pursuance of, or having the force of, an Act of Parliament, shall be deemed to be an enactment within the meaning of this section.

(3) Nothing in this Act shall affect Bills relating to the divorce or marriage of individuals, and any such Bill shall be introduced and proceed in Parliament in like manner as if this Act had not passed.

34. The local authority for any county or borough or other area shall not borrow money without either—

(a) special authority from the Irish Legislature, or

(b) the sanction of the proper department of the Irish Government:

and shall not, without such special authority, borrow;

(i) in the case of a municipal borough or town or area less than a county, any loan which together with the then outstanding debt of the local authority, will exceed twice the annual rateable value of the property in the municipal borough, town, or area; or

(ii) in the case of a country or larger area, any loan which together with the then outstanding debt of the local authority, will exceed one-tenth of the annual rateable value of the property in the county or area; or

(iii) in any case a loan exceeding one-half of the above limits without a local inquiry held in the county, borough, or area by a person appointed for the purpose by the said department.

Transitory Provisions

35.—(1) During *three* years from the passing of this Act, and if Parliament is then sitting until the end of that session of Parliament, the Irish Legislature shall not pass an Act respecting the relations of landlord and tenant, or the sale, purchase, or letting of land generally: Provided that nothing in this section shall prevent the passing of any Irish Act with a view to the purchase of land for railways, harbours, waterworks, town improvements, or other local undertakings.

(2) During *six* years from the passing of this Act, the appointment of a judge of the Supreme Court or other superior courts in Ireland (other than one of the Exchequer judges) shall be made in pursuance of a warrant from Her Majesty countersigned as heretofore.

36.—(1) Subject to the provisions of this Act Her Majesty the Queen in Council may make or direct such arrangements as seem necessary or proper for setting in motion the Irish Legislature and Government and for otherwise bringing this Act into operation.

(2) The Irish Legislature shall be summoned to meet on the *first Tuesday in September, one thousand eight hundred and ninety-four*, and the first election of members of the two Houses of the Irish Legislature shall be held at such time before that day, as may be fixed by Her Majesty in Council.

(3) Upon the first meeting of the Irish Legislature the members of the House of Commons then sitting for Irish constituencies, including the members for Dublin University, shall vacate their seats, and writs shall, as soon as conveniently may be, be issued by the Lord Chancellor of Ireland for the purpose of holding an election of members to serve in Parliament for the

constituencies named in the Second Schedule of this Act.

(4) The existing Chief Baron of the Exchequer, and the senior of the existing puisne judges of the Exchequer Division of the Supreme Court, or if they or either of them are or is dead or unable or unwilling to act, such other of the judges of the Supreme Court as Her Majesty may appoint, shall be the first Exchequer judges.

(5) Where it appears to Her Majesty the Queen in Council, before the expiration of *one year* after the appointed day, that any existing enactment respecting matters within the powers of the Irish Legislature requires adaptation to Ireland, whether—

(a) by the substitution of the Lord Lieutenant in Council, or of any department or officer of the executive Government in Ireland, for Her Majesty in Council, a Secretary of State, the Treasury, the Postmaster-General, the Board of Inland Revenue, or other public department or officer in Great Britain; or

(b) by the substitution of the Irish Consolidated Fund or moneys provided by the Irish Legislature for the Consolidated Fund of the United Kingdom, or moneys provided by Parliament; or

(c) by the substitution or confirmation by, or other act to be done by or to, the Irish Legislature for confirmation by or other act to be done by or to Parliament; or

(d) by any other adaptation; Her Majesty, by Order in Council, may make that adaptation.

(6) Her Majesty the Queen in Council may provide for the transfer of such property, rights, and liabilities, and the doing of such other things as may appear to Her Majesty necessary or proper for carrying into effect this Act or any Order in Council under this Act.

(7) An Order in Council under this section may make an adaptation or provide for a transfer either unconditionally or subject to such exceptions, conditions, and restrictions as may seem expedient.

(8) The draft of every Order in Council under this section shall be laid before both Houses of Parliament for not less than two months before it is made, and such Order when made shall, subject as respects Ireland to the provisions of an Irish Act, have full effect, but shall not interfere with the continued application to any place, authority, person, or thing, not in Ireland, of the enactment to which the Order relates.

37. Except as otherwise provided by this Act, all existing laws, institutions,

authorities, and officers in Ireland, whether judicial, administrative, or ministerial, and all existing taxes in Ireland shall continue as if this Act had not passed, but with the modifications necessary for adapting the same to this Act, and subject to be repealed, abolished, altered, and adapted in the manner and to the extent authorised by this Act.

38. Subject as in this Act mentioned the appointed day for the purposes of this Act shall be the day of the first meeting of the Irish Legislature, or such other day not more than *seven* months earlier or later as may be fixed by order of Her Majesty in Council either generally or with reference to any particular provision of this Act, and different days may be appointed for different purposes and different provisions of this Act, whether contained in the same section or in different sections.

39. In this Act unless the context otherwise requires—The expression 'existing' means existing at the passing of this Act.

The expression 'constituency' means a parliamentary constituency or a county or borough returning a member or members to serve in either House of the Irish Legislature, as the case requires, and the expression 'parliamentary constituency' means any county, borough, or university returning a member or members to serve in Parliament.

The expression 'parliamentary elector' means a person entitled to be registered as a voter at a parliamentary election.

The expression 'parliamentary election' means the election of a member to serve in Parliament.

The expression 'tax' includes duties and fees, and the expression 'duties of excise' does not include licence duties.

The expression 'foreign mails' means all postal packets, whether letters, parcels, or other packets, posted in the United Kingdom and sent to a place out of the United Kingdom, or posted in a place out of the United Kingdom and sent to a place in the United Kingdom, or in transit through the United Kingdom to a place out of the United Kingdom.

The expression 'telegraphic line' has the same meaning as in the Telegraph Acts, 1863 to 1892.

The expression 'duties on postage' includes all rates and sums chargeable for or in respect of postal packets, money orders, or telegrams, or otherwise under the Post Office Acts or the Telegraph Act, 1892.

The expression 'Irish Act' means a law made by the Irish Legislature.

The expression 'election laws' means the laws relating to the election of members to serve in Parliament, other than those relating to the qualification of electors, and includes all the laws respecting the registration of electors, the issue and execution of writs, the creation of polling districts, the taking of the poll, the questioning of elections, corrupt and illegal practices, the disqualification of members and the vacating of seats.

The expression 'rateable value' means the annual rateable value under the Irish Valuation Acts.

The expression 'salary' includes remuneration, allowances, and emoluments.

The expression 'pension' includes superannuation allowance.

40. This Act may be cited as the Irish Government Act, 1893.

Schedules

First Schedule

Legislative Council

Constituencies And Number OfCouncillors

Constituencies	Councillors
Antrim county	Three
Armagh county	One
Belfast borough	Two
Carlow county	One
Cavan county	One
Clare county	One
Cork county—	
East Riding	Three
West Riding	One
Cork borough	One
Donegal county	One
Down county	Three
Dublin county	Three
Dublin borough	Two
Fermanagh county	One
Galway county	Two

Kerry county	One
Kildare county	One
Kilkenny county	One
King's county	One
Leitrim and Sligo counties	One
Limerick county	Two
Londonderry county	One
Longford county	One
Louth county	One
Mayo county	One
Meath county	One
Monaghan county	One
Queen's county	One
Roscommon county	One
Tipperary county	Two
Tyrone county	One
Waterford county	One
Westmeath county	One
Wexford county	One
Wicklow county	One
	Forty-eight

The expression 'borough' in this Schedule means an existing parliamentary borough.

Counties of cities and towns not named in this Schedule shall be combined with the county at large in which they are included for parliamentary elections, and, if not so included, then with the county at large bearing the same name.

A borough named in this Schedule shall not for the purposes of this Schedule form part of any other constituency.

Second Schedule

Irish Members In The House Of Commons

Constituencies	Number of Members for House of Commons
Antrim county	Three
Armagh county	Two
Belfast borough (in divisions as mentioned below)	Four
Carlow county	One
Cavan county	Two
Clare county	Two
Cork county (in divisions as mentioned below)	Five
Cork borough	Two
Donegal county	Three
Down county	Three
Dublin county	Two
Dublin borough (in divisions as mentioned below)	Four
Fermanagh county	One
Galway county	Three
Galway borough	One
Kerry county	Three
Kildare county	One
Kilkenny county	One
Kilkenny borough	One
King's county	One
Leitrim county	Two
Limerick county	Two
Limerick borough	One
Londonderry county	Two
Londonderry borough	One
Longford county	One
Louth county	One
Mayo county	Three
Meath county	Two

Monaghan county	Two
Newry borough	One
Queen's county	One
Roscommon county	Two
Sligo county	Two
Tipperary county	Three
Tyrone county	Three
Waterford county	One
Waterford borough	One
Westmeath county	One
Wexford county	Two
Wicklow county	One
	Eighty

(1) In this Schedule the expression 'borough' means an existing parliamentary borough.

(2) In the parliamentary boroughs of Belfast and Dublin, one member shall be returned by each of the existing parliamentary divisions of those boroughs, and the law relating to the divisions of boroughs shall apply accordingly.

(3) The county of Cork shall be divided into two divisions, consisting of the East Riding and the West Riding, and three members shall be elected by the East Riding, and two members shall be elected by the West Riding; and the law relating to divisions of counties shall apply to those divisions.

Third Schedule

Finance

Imperial Liabilities, Expenditure, And Miscellaneous Revenue

Liabilities

For the purposes of this Act 'Imperial liabilities' consist of:—

(1) The funded and unfunded debt of the United Kingdom, inclusive of terminable annuities paid out of the permanent annual charge for the National Debt, and inclusive of the cost of the management of the said funded and unfunded debt, but exclusive of the Local Loans stock and Guaranteed Land

stock and the cost of the management thereof; and

(2) All other charges on the Consolidated Fund of the United Kingdom for the repayment of borrowed money, or to fulfil a guarantee.

Expenditure

For the purpose of this Act Imperial expenditure consists of expenditure for the following services:—

I. Naval and military expenditure (including Greenwich Hospital).

II. Civil expenditure, that is to say—

(a) Civil list and Royal family.

(b) Salaries, pensions, allowances, and incidental expenses of—

(i) Lord Lieutenant of Ireland;

(ii) Exchequer judges in Ireland.

(c) Building, works, salaries, pensions, printing, stationery, allowances, and incidental expenses of—

(i) Parliament;

(ii) National Debt Commissioners;

(iii) Foreign Office and diplomatic and consular service, including secret service, special services, and telegraph subsidies;

(iv) Colonial Office, including special services and telegraph subsidies;

(v) Privy Council;

(vi) Board of Trade, including the Mercantile Marine Fund, Patent Office, Railway Commission, and Wreck Commission, but excluding Bankruptcy;

(vii) Mint;

(viii) Meteorological Society;

(ix) Slave trade service.

(d) Foreign mails and telegraphic communication with places outside the United Kingdom.

Revenue

For the purposes of this Act the public revenue to a portion of which Ireland may claim to be entitled consists of revenue from the following sources:—

1. Suez Canal shares or payments on account thereof.

2. Loans and advances to foreign countries.

3. Annual payments by British possessions.

4. Fees, stamps, and extra receipts received by departments, the expenses of which are part of the Imperial expenditure.

5. Small branches of the hereditary revenues of the Crown.

6. Foreshores.

[The Fourth, Fifth, Sixth, and Seventh Schedules are for the saving of space omitted.]

Lightning Source UK Ltd.
Milton Keynes UK
UKHW040820020123
414708UK00004B/325

9 783752 308761